MAGAZINE PRESENTS

BRAIN TWISTERS

from the

WORLD PUZZLE CHAMPIONSHIPS

VOLUME 2

EDITED BY WILL SHORTZ AND RON OSHER

TIMES

BOOKS

ISBN 0-8129-2616-1

Manufactured in the United States of America

9 8 7 6 5 4 3 2

First Edition

CONTENTS

Introduction .5

Foreword 7

U.S./CANADA QUALIFYING TEST

Going Halfsies 11

Try-Angles 11

Time Share 12

Freeway Frenzy 12

Common Elements 13

Step By Step 14

Digititis 14

Word Search 15

Robot 1 15

Robot 2 15

Boxed In .16

Tall Tale 16

On Our Honor 17

Going In Circles 17

Crisscross 18

A Perfect Match 19

Sister Carrie 19

Trial Separation 20

Key Decision 20

Spelling Checker 21

Times After Times 21

Year's End 22

Cross-Link 22

Pi Chart 1 23

Pi Chart 2 23

Path Marks 24

Completely Out Of Shape 24

Race For The Gold 25

SECOND WORLD PUZZLE CHAMPIONSHIP

Ladybugs 27

Minicross 27

Picture Logic 28

Counting Squares 28

Find Your Way 29

Snowflakes 30

Domino Theory I 31

Find The Pair 32

Town Square 33

Battleships 34

Warm-Up 35

Battleships 1 36

Battleships 2 37

Battleships 3 38

Battleships 4 39

Logical Labyrinth 40

Swimmers 41

Leaves 42

CONTENTS

Reader 43

Soccer 1 44

How Many? 45

Jumping 46

Lighthouses 48

Lighthouses 1 49

Lighthouses 2 50

Two-Way Anagrams 51

Multiplication Puzzle 52

Do You Speak Esperanto? 53

International Crossword Puzzle . . . 54

Numerical Pentamino 55

Eight Is Enough 55

Monitor On The Blink 56

Four Moving Points 57

The Multiplication Pyramid 58

The Multiplication Pyramid 59

Ten Flowers 60

Lady Sings The Blues 61

Diamond Treasure 62

Diamond Treasure 1 63

Diamond Treasure 2 63

Diamond Treasure 3 64

Diamond Treasure 4 64

Diamond Treasure 5 65

Diamond Treasure 6 65

Magic Squares (Czech Style) 66

THIRD WORLD PUZZLE CHAMPIONSHIP

Anagrams 1 67

Anagrams 2 68

Homage To Kafka 69

Pyramid Power 1 70

Mirror, Mirror 71

Domino Theory 2 72

Downtown The Easy Way 73

Downtown The Hard Way 74

Soccer 2 75

Not In My Neighborhood! 76

Chain Gang 77

Divide And Conquer 78

Post Office 79

Summing Up 80

Car Quest 81

Square Sum 82

Not So Square Sum 82

Pyramid Power 2 83

Calling The Game 83

Give 'Em The Works 84

Keep Away 86

Answers 87

INTRODUCTION

The contestants and officials were having lunch at the 3rd World Puzzle Championship in Germany in 1994 when we heard a crash and a clatter. Looking up in surprise, we saw the host and organizer of the event, Andreas Franz, lying flat on the floor. He had tripped while walking through the dining room, spilling a trayful of tableware in front of him.

I vaguely noted the peculiar shirt he was wearing: all white, except for three large variously colored patches (a circle, a square, and a triangle) positioned on the front and back. What none of us realized was that the tableware spill wasn't accidental. It was a pretext to get our attention. That afternoon at the championship every team was given a white shirt, a container of straight pins, and an array of colored patches and asked to reproduce the shirt seen at lunch!

This surprise test gives a slight taste of the World Puzzle Championship, an annual event first held in New York City in 1992, which draws together puzzle enthusiasts from around the world for several days of lively mental competition. Each country is represented by a four-person team, selected via a national contest or some other means, who tackle a wide assortment of puzzles both individually and as a group. All the challenges are language and cultural neutral to the maximum extent possible. Besides tests of memory (as in the above example), there are number puzzles, logic problems, visual teasers, crisscross and word search puzzles (using a variety of languages), hands-on mechanical puzzles, geography quizzes, and so on. No crossword or standard word puzzles permitted.

The best of these challenges from the 1993 and '94 world championships have been collected in this volume, along with the complete 1993 U.S./Canadian team qualifying test, so you can see if you have the stuff of which puzzle championships are made.

This is a unusual book, because, first of all, it doesn't contain the sorts of mental tests you commonly encounter in puzzle books and magazines. Many of them are brand new types, or types popular elsewhere in the world but not previously introduced here. Some are based on one-of-a-kind ideas.

The book is also unusual in that, if you wish, you really can use it to see how you stack up mentally with the world's greatest puzzle solvers.

We would like to thank the organizers of the 2nd and 3rd World Puzzle Championships—Vitezslav Koudelka, editor-in-chief of Kira Publishing Co., Brno, Czech Republic; and Andreas Franz, chief puzzle editor of Bastei-Verlag, Bergisch Gladbach, Germany—for permission to publish the puzzles from their respective tournaments. U.S. team member and 1994 World Puzzle Champion Ron Osher selected and edited these puzzles for the book.

Thanks also to GAMES magazine, of which I was formerly the editor, for helping found the championship in 1992; Stanley Newman and Times Books for providing the U.S. teams with financial support; and Lufthansa for providing international travel.

As I write this, annual World Puzzle Championships continue to be planned, in Romania in 1995 and other countries thereafter. News and reports on them can be found in GAMES and on the Internet. To receive direct notification of future national qualifying tests, please write: World Puzzle Championship, Times Books, 201 E. 50th St., New York, NY 10022.

But first, try your hand on these puzzles. Sorry, the shirt test couldn't be included!

Will Shortz

WPC founder and director, 1992

U.S. team captain, 1993-94

1993 RESULTS

TOP 10 TEAMS

1	Czech Republic	2,609
2	USA	2,499
3	Canada	2,192
4	Poland	2,172
5	Japan	2,128
6	Turkey	2,064
7	Hungary	1,927
8	Slovakia	1,898
9	Argentina	1,856
10	Croatia	1,623

TOP 10 INDIVIDUALS

1	Robert Babilon	Czech Republic
2	Wei-Hwa Huang	USA
3	Pavel Kalhous	Czech Republic
4	Ron Osher	USA
5	Kamer Alyanakyan	Turkey
6	Dan Johnson	USA
7	Julian West	Canada
tie	Michal Stajszczak	Poland
9	David Samuel	Canada
10	Pablo Milrud	Argentina

1994 RESULTS

TOP 10 TEAMS

1	Czech Republic	13,986
2	USA	13,753
3	Croatia	13,151
4	Slovakia	12,090
5	Germany	12,027
6	Hungary	11,449
7	Finland	11,409
8	Turkey	10,560
9	Poland	10,130
10	Slovenia	10,114

TOP 10 INDIVIDUALS

1	Ron Osher	USA
2	Pavel Kalhous	Czech Republic
3	Pero Galogaza	Croatia
4	Boris Nazanaky	Croatia
5	Markus Gegenheimer	Germany
6	Zdenek Vokicka	Czech Republic
7	Wei-Hwa Huang	USA
8	Robert Bablion	Czech Republic
9	Kamer Alyanakyan	Turkey
10	Luka Pavicic	Croatia

FOREWORD

When Will Shortz was planning the first World Puzzle Championship, he asked me, formerly the host of several American puzzle conventions, to be the host/coordinator of this international event. There would be about 100 visitors who would need to be lodged, fed, entertained, and transported. Since I love puzzles, talking, and traveling, this was an offer I couldn't refuse. The fact that I would be getting paid to do all this was just icing on the cake.

I didn't know what to expect. Much to my sons' dismay, I have no trouble walking into a room filled with strangers and talking to anyone about anything. But I was a little nervous about this. Except for the American and Canadian teams, no one spoke English as a first language. Would the same rules apply? How could I make people feel at ease if I couldn't speak to them?

I needn't have worried. As I stood at the welcoming table at New York University's Weinstein Hall, I discovered several things: Most of the contestants spoke English, a smile was an international language of its own, and I could get over a lot of awkwardness by piling people up with information packets, keys, and food.

Between puzzling, sightseeing, traveling, eating, and partying the four days of the competition just whizzed by. At the end of the event I needed two things desperately: sleep and a bigger Rolodex to add all the names and addresses of my new friends.

Those friendships have aged well since 1992 when the WPC began. Now we seek each other out at the competitions and correspond regularly throughout the year. I've visited my friends in Brno and Amsterdam where they took me to places I'd never have found on my own. I've had visitors from Czech Republic, the Netherlands, Germany, and Ukraine stay with me or break bread at my house. I've toured New York City with these friends and shown them my favorite places around town.

I feel so lucky to have friends of all ages. Some of them are close to my age while others are a lot younger than I am—some just barely older than my sons. But age doesn't seem to matter. We started with a common interest—puzzles. We're curious about what we do, how we create, how we think, and how we solve. But we also like each other and discovered that while our languages and lifestyles may be different, puzzling cuts through all barriers and enables us to see the similarities in our lives.

Helene Hovanec

WPC Host, 1992

Judging Panel Chairwoman, 1993-1994

The 13 teams hard at work on the puzzles in the Second World Puzzle Championship in Brno, Czech Republic.

The 1993 US Team working together on a "Grecian Urn" jigsaw. Left to Right: Ron Osher, Larry Baum, Wei-Hwa Huang and Dan Johnson.

THE WORLD PUZZLE CHAMPIONSHIPS

The 1993 Canadian Team. Left to Right: David Samuel, Darren Rigby, Marie Vasilou, Julian West and Mark Danna of GAMES Magazine (Honorary Captain).

The 1994 US Team. Left to Right: Messrs. Osher, Huang, Baum and Johnson.

US Team Captain Will Shortz standing in front of the *MS Britannia*, the cruise ship that hosted the Third World Puzzle Championship in Germany.

The three top scorers in the Third World Puzzle Championship. Left to Right: Pavel Kalhous, Czech Republic (2nd place), Ron Osher, US (1st place – the World Puzzle Champion), Pero Galogaza, Croatia (3rd place).

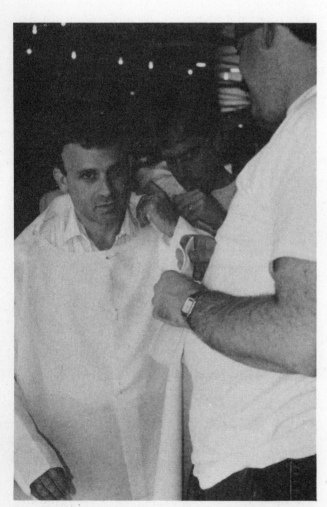

Messrs. Baum, Osher and Johnson piecing together the shirt puzzle cited on page 5.

The 1994 US contingent standing in front of Germany's Marksburg Castle.

U.S./CANADA QUALIFYING TEST

Before tackling the World Championship caliber puzzles, let's see if you qualify! On the next 15 pages you will find the test used to select the U.S. and Canadian representatives to the 2nd World Puzzle Championship. Created by GAMES magazine staff and other contributors under the direction of Will Shortz, it was administered by fax in May 1993. At a preselected time, 185 contestants in 185 different locations received the 34 puzzles. A short two hours later the answers were due by return fax.

These puzzles were specifically created to be language and culture neutral in order to best simulate the World Championship conditions. The degree of difficulty varies. So if you are stumped by one, feel free to move on and come back later. In the actual fax contest, no one solved all the puzzles in the time allotted, but go ahead and try. You might be the first!

SCORING

The point values range from 5 to 20 points and are listed next to each puzzle. For each correct answer add the number of points indicated. For incorrect answers, the first two are on the house (no penalty is assessed). After that, subtract the point value indicated for that puzzle from your total score. When scoring penalties, consider mistakes in order from the first puzzle to the last.

ALTERNATE SCORING METHOD

Of course, competition is not for everybody. So, under the alternate scoring method, take as much time as you want, forget about points, and enjoy!

GOING HALFSIES

Divide this grid into two parts so that the sum of the numbers in each part is equal.   *5 points*

1	2	3	4
5	6	7	8
9	10	11	12

TRY-ANGLES

How many triangles are in this design?   *10 points*

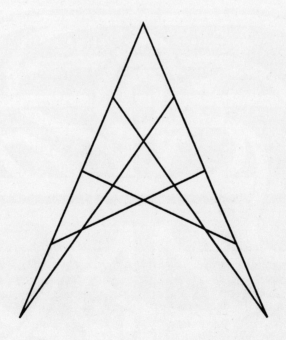

TIME SHARE

During a 24-hour period, which segment of a digit on a 12-hour digital clock remains on the longest *without interruption?* The 10 digits are shown below. Circle the correct segment.   *5 points*

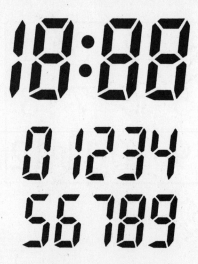

FREEWAY FRENZY

There are six cars stalled on this complicated freeway interchange. What is the maximum number of cars you can avoid, while entering and exiting the freeway where indicated by the arrows? No sharp turns allowed.   *10 points*

COMMON ELEMENTS

The items in each of the seven sets below have some unusual property in common. Find one object (a-h) in the box at right that best shares that property. One object will be left over when you're done.   *5 points each*

STEP BY STEP

Number the following steps from 1 to 10 in the order that you must do them
to solve and complete this puzzle.   *10 points*

___ Put a "1" next to it.
___ Put the lowest number not yet used next to it.
___ Read all the choices.
___ Double-check that you haven't made a copying error.
___ Read all the choices that don't have numbers next to them.
___ If you haven't yet placed a "10," repeat the preceding three steps.
___ Read the instructions.
___ Copy the numbers, in order, onto the answer line below.
___ Determine which of those is earliest.
___ Determine which is first.

Answer: _____

DIGITITIS

We've replaced all but a few of the digits in the long division problem below.
Replace the numbers, one digit per dash, so that the completed division is correct.
What is the quotient (the top number in the solution)?   *20 points*

WORD SEARCH

Find the 23 four-letter geographical names in the grid below. Each name can read in any direction horizontally, vertically or diagonally. When all the names have been found, the eight unused letters can themselves be rearranged to spell two related four-letter geographical names. What are they?   *10 points*

ARNO	OISE
ASIA	OMAN
FIJI	OMSK
GAZA	ORAN
HILO	OSLO
IOWA	ROMA
IRAN	SAAR
JAVA	TOGO
KOBE	UTAH
NICE	WACO
OAHU	WIEN
OHIO	

```
M  E  B  O  K  S  M  O
E  N  I  C  E  U  C  N
S  O  A  O  R  A  N  A
O  A  I  R  W  V  R  M
G  H  A  S  I  A  O  O
O  A  P  R  E  J  L  R
T  T  Z  I  N  S  I  A
L  U  H  A  O  O  H  F
```

ROBOT 1

How many cubes make up this symmetrically built robot?   *5 points*

ROBOT 2

And what is the surface area of this robot, counting each side of a cube as a 1x1 unit?   *10 points*

BOXED IN

Six of the seven lettered pieces (A–G) shown at right can be joined together to make the 6x6 square shown below. Pieces may be rotated but not flipped. Which piece is not used?   *15 points*

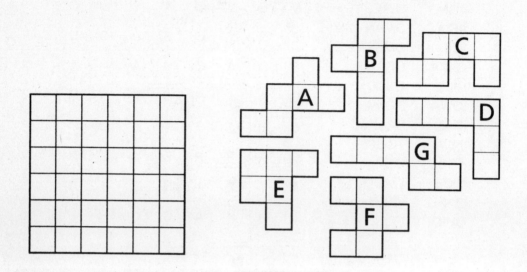

TALL TALE

Kim is shorter than Joyce, but Kim's not the shortest person on the basketball team. In fact, Kim is shorter than those who are at least as tall as Amy (including Amy herself), and taller than everyone else.

Flo is taller than Lisa, but Flo's not the tallest person on the team. In fact Flo is taller than those who are at least as short as Amy (including Amy herself), and shorter than everyone else.

Everyone is a different height. From tallest to shortest, what is the order of the heights for Amy, Flo, Joyce, Kim and Lisa?   *10 points*

ON OUR HONOR

The 16 honor cards in a deck of cards have been laid out below, but except for the ace at the upper left, all their values have been omitted. Using the clues at the beginning of the rows and columns, complete the tableau.   *10 points*

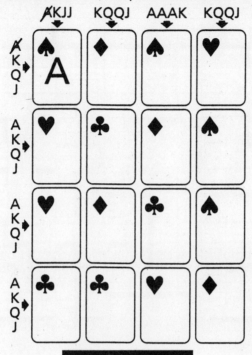

GOING IN CIRCLES

Place the numbers 1 through 9 in the spaces so that the total is the same in each of the five circles and center column.   *20 points*

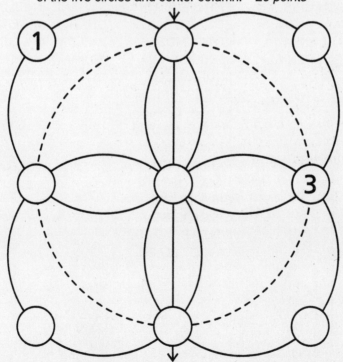

CRISSCROSS

Fit *either* the first or the last name of each celebrity below into the crisscross grid. When the puzzle is done, the names of three people (one for each answer length) will be left over. Who are they?   *20 points*

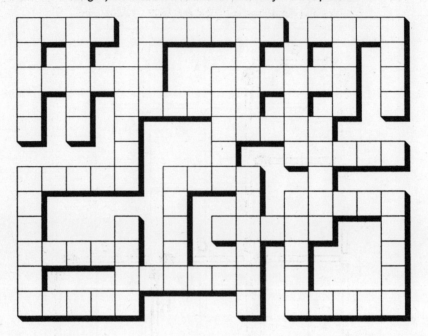

4	5	6
ABBA EBAN	ALVIN AILEY	ARNOLD PALMER
ALDO MORO	ANWAR SADAT	BLAISE PASCAL
CARL JUNG	BRYAN ADAMS	DANIEL ORTEGA
JOAN MIRO	CARLO PONTI	ENRICO CARUSO
LEON URIS	CHRIS EVERT	EUGENE O'NEILL
MATA HARI	EDGAR DEGAS	GRAHAM GREENE
PAUL ANKA	EDWIN MOSES	IMELDA MARCOS
SEAN PENN	JESSE OWENS	INDIRA GANDHI
	LOUIS MALLE	
	MARIE CURIE	
	MOSHE DAYAN	
	OSCAR WILDE	
	PAAVO NURMI	
	PAULA ABDUL	
	ROGER MOORE	
	SEIJI OZAWA	
	SIMON LEBON	
	SONIA BRAGA	
	WOODY ALLEN	

A PERFECT MATCH

Move exactly two lettered matchsticks to new positions to leave just four squares instead of the five currently shown. (You are *not* allowed to move the unlettered matches.) Your solution must not have any leftover matches that are not part of a square. Which two matches must be moved?   *10 points*

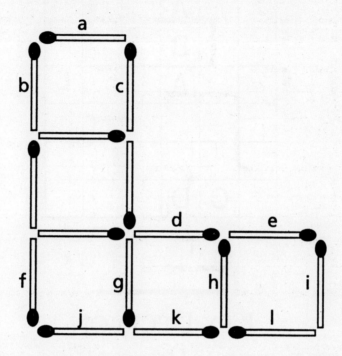

SISTER CARRIE

At the Hurstwood Retirement Home, octogenarian Carrie Meeber has invited her five siblings to her room for one of her notorious birthday parties. The youngest person at the party is 83, the oldest is 88, and no two are the same age in full years. Assign Carrie and her siblings their respective ages.   *10 points*

1. Carrie isn't the oldest, but she's older than Harry and Tom.

2. Brenda and Carrie are more than one year apart in age, as are Carrie and Laura, as are Laura and Dick.

3. The sum of Carrie's and Dick's ages is the same as the sum of Laura's and Tom's ages.

TRIAL SEPARATION

Divide the grid into four parts—each the same size and shape—so that all four letters of the alphabet are separated (and the two A's are together).   *15 points*

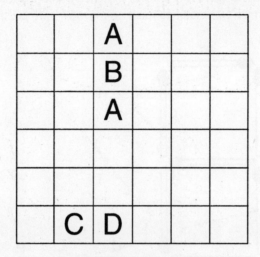

KEY DECISION

You have seven keys numbered 1 to 7, each of which will unlock all correspondingly numbered doors in the dungeon below. Which three keys will allow you to pass from the upper left room to the lower right?   *15 points*

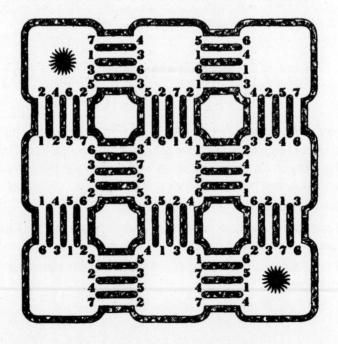

SPELLING CHECKER

Place one letter in each circle below so that the name TOMAS DE TORQUEMADA (head of the Spanish Inquisition) can be read in a series of consecutively connected circles.   *10 points*

TOMASDETORQUEMADA

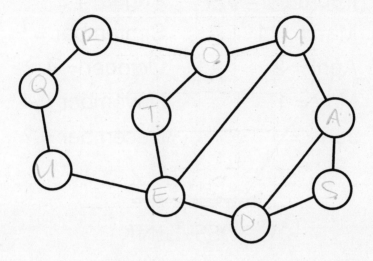

TIMES AFTER TIMES

The arithmetic operation below uses all the digits from 1 to 9 once each. Find another such operation in which the center is not 156.   *20 points*

$$\boxed{2} \times \boxed{7}\boxed{8} = \boxed{1}\boxed{5}\boxed{6} = \boxed{4} \times \boxed{3}\boxed{9}$$

$$\Box \times \Box\Box = \Box\Box\Box = \Box \times \Box\Box$$

YEAR'S END

What number completes the relationship? *15 points*

January = 2	July = 0
February = 3	August = 2
March = 1	September = 5
April = 2	October = 4
May = 1	November = 4
June = 1	December = ?

CROSS-LINK

Connect the two dots at the top and the bottom of the figure with a continuous line by moving from square to adjacent square, up, down, left, or right (but not diagonally). The number at the beginning of every row and column indicates exactly how many of the squares in that row or column the lines must pass through. No square may be visited more than once. *15 points*

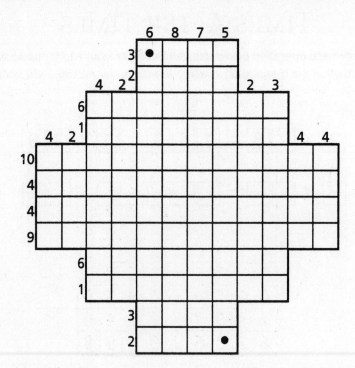

PI CHART 1

The 9x9 square below lists π to 81 digits. Find a continuous path of 10 digits, each in a different square, that adds up to the highest total. The path may proceed horizontally and vertically, but not diagonally. What is that total?   *10 points*

3	1	4	1	5	9	2	6	5
3	5	8	9	7	9	3	2	3
8	4	6	2	6	4	3	3	8
3	2	7	9	5	0	2	8	8
4	1	9	7	1	6	9	3	9
9	3	7	5	1	0	5	8	2
0	9	7	4	9	4	4	5	9
2	3	0	7	8	1	6	4	0
6	2	8	6	2	0	8	9	9

PI CHART 2

Now find a continuous path of 10 digits, each in a different square, that adds up to the *lowest* total. Again, the path may proceed horizontally and vertically, but not diagonally. What is the total?   *10 points*

3	1	4	1	5	9	2	6	5
3	5	8	9	7	9	3	2	3
8	4	6	2	6	4	3	3	8
3	2	7	9	5	0	2	8	8
4	1	9	7	1	6	9	3	9
9	3	7	5	1	0	5	8	2
0	9	7	4	9	4	4	5	9
2	3	0	7	8	1	6	4	0
6	2	8	6	2	0	8	9	9

PATH MARKS

How many ways are there to go from Start to Finish passing through exactly six intersections, all of which have different letters? Do not repeat an intersection with any given path. *20 points*

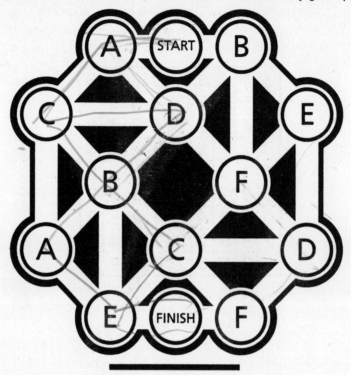

COMPLETELY OUT OF SHAPE

This pentagon with lines connecting all the vertices consists of 20 individual line segments as shown. What is the least number of them that must be deleted so that no triangle of any size remains? *15 points*

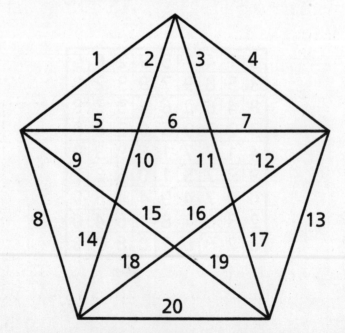

RACE FOR THE GOLD

Below are the names of 29 track and field gold medalists at the 1992 Olympics. Fit as many of them into a 5x5 grid as possible. Several grids appear below for your convenience. Each name you use must be spelled out in a chain of connected squares, traveling horizontally, vertically, or diagonally, not necessarily in a straight line. A square may be repeated within a word.

Score 2 points for using 7 names; 4 points for 8 names; 6 points for 9 names;
8 points for 10 names; 16 points for 11 names; 28 points for 12 names;
42 points for 13 names; and 62 points for 14 or more names.

ABDUVALIYEV	PERLOV
BIRIR	RENKE
BOULMERKA	ROMANOVA
CHRISTIE	RUIZ
CONLEY	SKAH
DEVERS	SOTOMAYOR
DRECHSLER	STUICE
GARCIA	TANUI
HENKEL	TULU
HWANG	UBARTAS
KRIVELEVA	YEGOROVA
LEWIS	YOUNG
MARSH	ZELEZNY
PATOULIDOU	ZMELIK
PEREC	

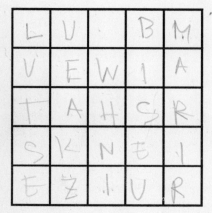

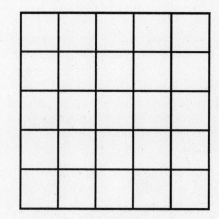

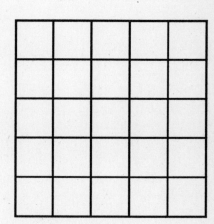

THE WORLD PUZZLE CHAMPIONSHIP

Now that you've qualified for the team, it's time for the championship puzzles themselves.

What follows are puzzles from the 2nd and 3rd World Puzzle Championships held in Brno, Czech Republic, and Cologne, Germany, respectively.

Not every puzzle was of the pencil and paper variety and could be reproduced here.

In Brno, for example, for one puzzle, a slide of a fruit stand and an arcade booth (filled with every kind of merchandise and paraphernalia) was projected on a screen for 60 seconds. Immediately following, one of the judges held up a series of items to be identified as having appeared on the screen or not.

In Cologne, the tournament was held aboard a cruise ship. One night, as we passed the famous Lorelei we were treated to a salute of gunfire from atop the fabled rock. The next day's challenges included knowing the number of shots that were fired!

On these pages you will find the best of those puzzles that lend themselves to the printed page. As before, if a puzzle seems too hard, come back to it later and see if with a clear head it's gotten any easier. If on the other hand they all seem easy, we want you for the team!

LADYBUGS

The ladybugs on the seven flowers have not been positioned at random, but according to a specific system. Work out this system and position the third ladybug on flower number 1.

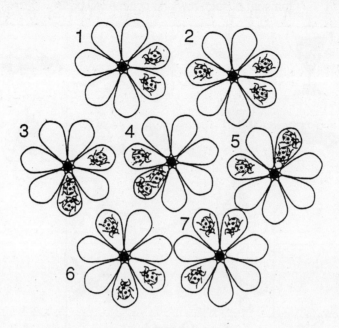

MINICROSS

Put the seven given numbers into the minicross diagram, so that the numbers cross correctly at the junction points.

01000   01100   01110   10001   10110   11100   11110

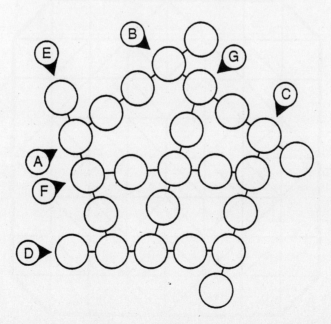

PICTURE LOGIC

Enter the correct pictures in the five empty squares fulfilling the following conditions:
If you correctly substitute the numbers 1 to 7 for individual pictures,
the sum of each row and column will be 21.

COUNTING SQUARES

How many squares are there in the diagram?

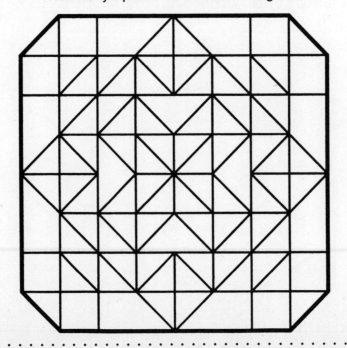

FIND YOUR WAY

Make your way from the top left-hand corner to the bottom right-hand corner passing through every empty square exactly once while moving horizontally and vertically but not diagonally.
Your path may not cross itself and you may not go through any houses.

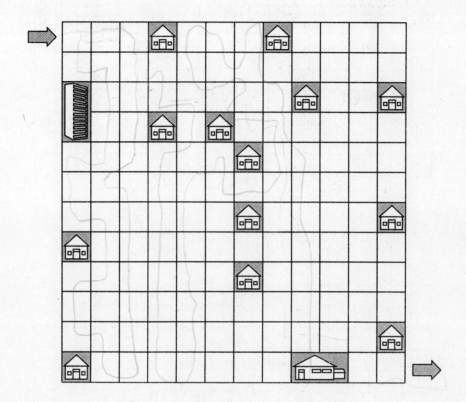

SNOWFLAKES

Snowflakes are positioned in four different-sized squares (A, B, C, D) according to a specific system.
Put your snowflakes into the empty square E, following the same system.

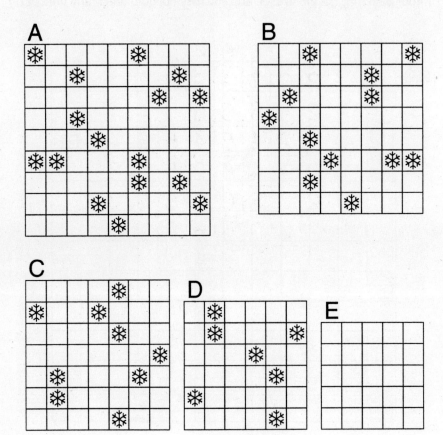

DOMINO THEORY I

Divide this diagram into the 28 dominoes shown below. No domino can be used twice, and none should be left out. Each individual domino can be placed in one of four possible positions (from left to right, from right to left, down from the top or up from the bottom).

```
      6 0 4 1
  3 2 1 1 3 3 1 1
  2 4 6 6 5 0 4 1
  3 2 1 5 4 5 5 4
  0 2 4 6 2 5 6 3
  2 0 3 6 0 5 5 3
  2 6 0 5 6 0 2 3
      0 4 4 1
```

0 0	1 1	2 2	3 3	4 4	5 5	6 6
0 1	1 2	2 3	3 4	4 5	5 6	
0 2	1 3	2 4	3 5	4 6		
0 3	1 4	2 5	3 6			
0 4	1 5	2 6				
0 5	1 6					
0 6						

FIND THE PAIR

Only two of the patterns of squares in the group below are exactly the same. You may rotate the entire pattern but may not make any other changes to find the matched set. Which two are they?

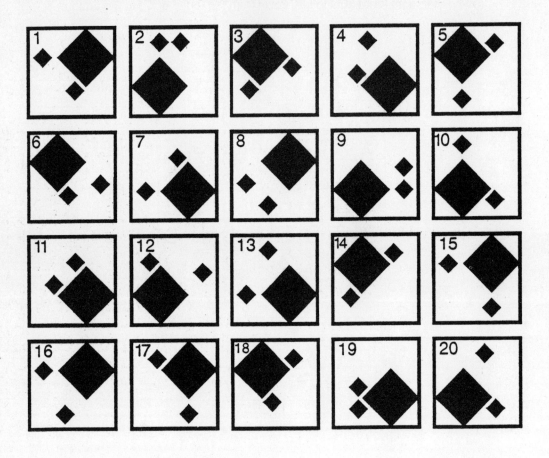

TOWN SQUARE

Partition the diagram of the town square below into the smallest possible number of square sections.
The lines must follow the square grid. The squares should not overlap.
Two grids have been provided for your convenience.

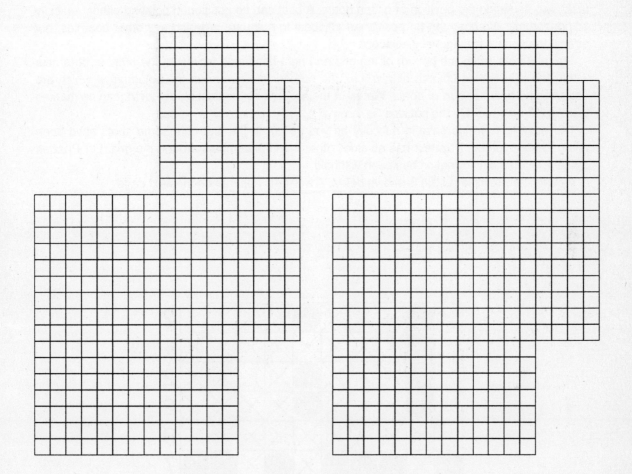

BATTLESHIPS

The battle at sea will be fought on a 10x10 grid representing the ocean. There are ten boats positioned on it: 1 battleship (takes up 4 squares); 2 cruisers (take up 3 squares each); 3 destroyers (2 squares each) and four submarines (which occupy 1 square each). The boats are marked on the diagram. Note that a submarine is represented by a shaded circle, the ends of boats by a rounded-off shaded square, and the middle of boats by a fully shaded square. Your task is to ascertain the position of all ten boats. A boat can be positioned pointing either vertically or horizontally. No boat can be positioned adjacent to a square in which any other boat lies, not even if the square is diagonally adjacent.

The numbers along the bottom of the grid and right-hand side represent the number of targets within the appropriate column or row, i.e., the number of squares in the column/row which are occupied by boats or part of boats. Water, or the squares not containing any boat, can be marked with an "X" as you solve the puzzles.

The puzzles here increase in difficulty as you go on. In the first one, some shots have been taken to start you off. Puzzle 2 has no clues other than the numbers around the grid. For Puzzles 3 and 4, even that information has been withheld.

A completed sample puzzle is shown below. A warm-up appears on the next page.

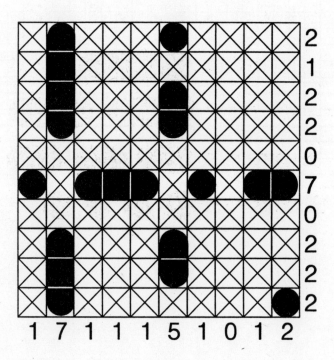

WARM-UP

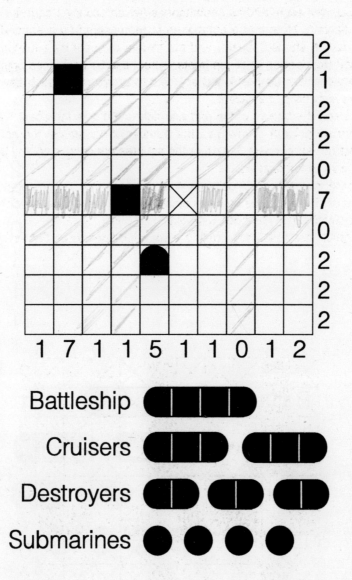

Battleship

Cruisers

Destroyers

Submarines

BATTLESHIPS 1

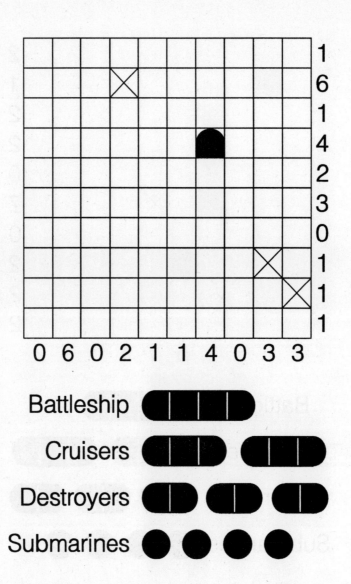

Battleship

Cruisers

Destroyers

Submarines

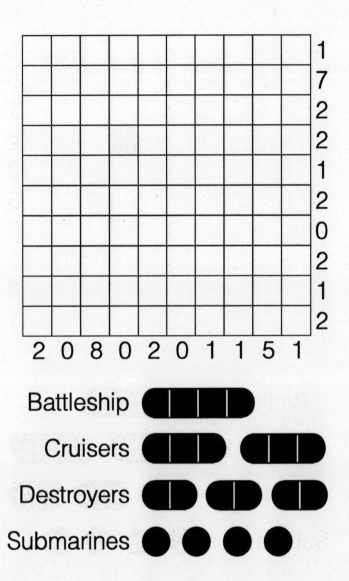

BATTLESHIPS 3

Believe it or not, this is enough information to solve.

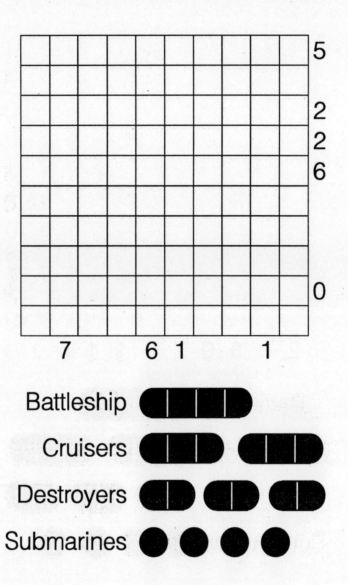

Battleship

Cruisers

Destroyers

Submarines

BATTLESHIPS 4

For words of encouragement, see Battleships 3.

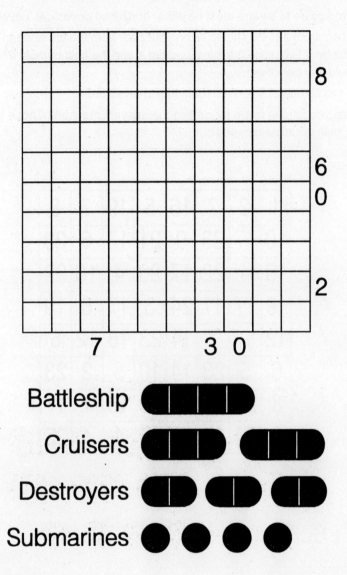

Battleship

Cruisers

Destroyers

Submarines

LOGICAL LABYRINTH

Find your way through the numerical labyrinth from the number 1 in the top left-hand corner to the number 25 in the bottom right-hand corner, obeying the following rules:

1. Movement from square to square must be either horizontal or vertical, never diagonal.

2. All of the numbers from 1 to 25 should lie on your path from the entrance to the exit of the maze. None of the numbers (including the initial number 1 and the final number 25) should be used twice, nor should any be left out.

3. The numbers 1 to 25 do not lie on the route in numerical order.

4. Mark your route through the maze by circling the relevant numbers. Those squares which do not lie on your path could be crossed out.

1	2	7	16	5	19	7	8
10	17	23	9	21	13	6	23
15	4	22	17	20	4	18	22
19	17	11	24	3	17	8	19
12	9	7	14	23	18	12	6
6	5	23	14	10	5	2	23
8	20	10	11	19	18	1	17
2	24	15	22	13	4	4	25

SWIMMERS

The diagram shows a swimming race at a point when four of the contestants have reached the end of the pool and are swimming back to the starting line. However, you do not know which four swimmers have already reached the end of the pool and have turned back, and which have yet to get there. The order in which the eight swimmers finished the race did not change from the order which they held at the given instant. No two swimmers in adjacent lanes of the pool finished the race one immediately after the other. None of the swimmers held a position in the final result table which was the same number as the number of their lane (for example the swimmer in the third lane did not come in third; the swimmer in lane six did not come in sixth; and so on). Find the order of finish for the swimmer in each lane.

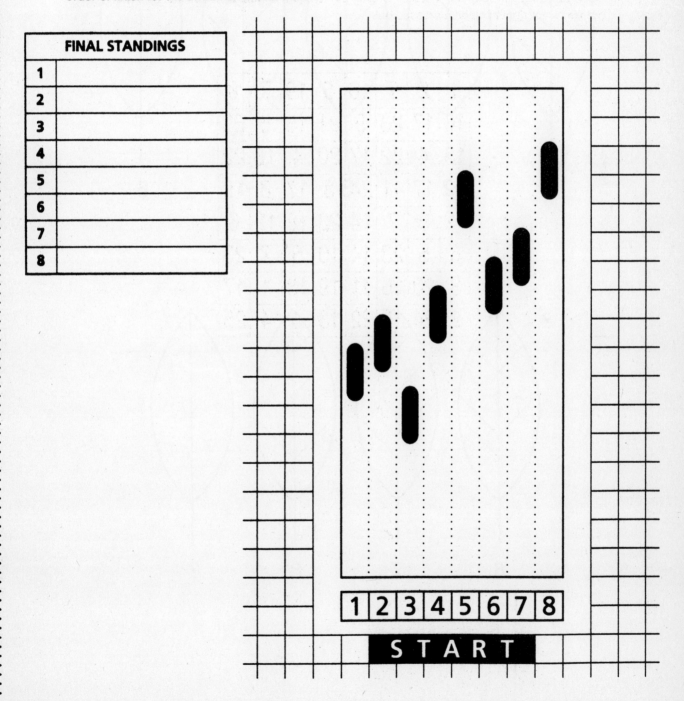

FINAL STANDINGS	
1	
2	
3	
4	
5	
6	
7	
8	

LEAVES

The veins on the individual leaves are arranged according to a definite system. Figure out the system and correctly draw the veins in the ninth leaf, so that the system is maintained.

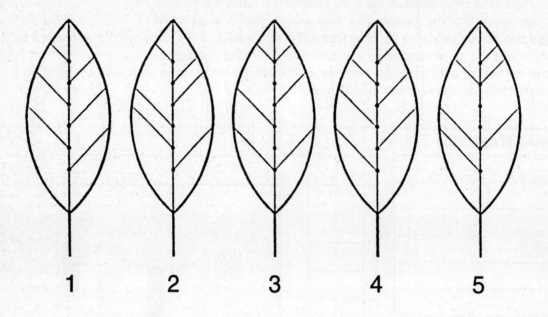

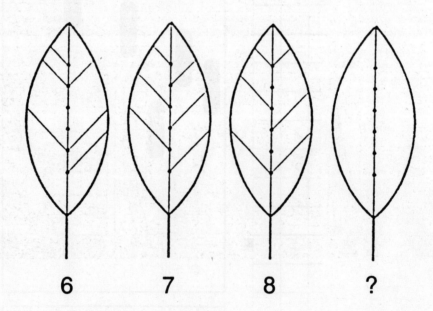

READER

Using the clues in each one, put the pictures in chronological order.

SOCCER 1

Soccer is one of the world's most popular and widespread sports. The diagram below shows a soccer field. Your task is to position the players for the scoring of two goals: one goal for the white team, and one goal for the black team. The goalkeeper kicks off from his goal to one of his teammates, who passes the ball to a further player and so on. All the players on a team should touch the ball. At the same time the following rules should not be broken:

1. The path of the ball from one player to another should be direct and no other player should stand in its way. Indicate this path with an arrow from one player to another;

2. A player can only pass the ball in one of the following eight directions: forwards (up), backwards (down), to the left or right, or diagonally (but only at a 45 degree angle);

3. Each player can have only one contact with the ball.

For ease of solution the soccer field is drawn on squared paper. First mark in the arrows showing the passes and goal of the white team and then those of the black team.

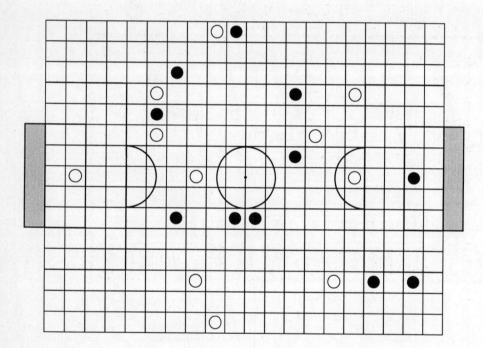
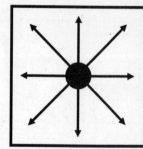

HOW MANY?

There are four squares here, with various objects in them.
How many of these objects appear in all four squares? Circle them.

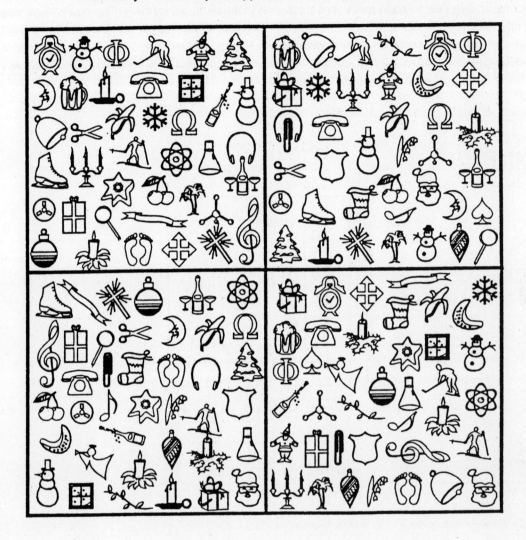

JUMPING

This numerical puzzle is in fact a game for one player. It is based on a concept thought up by the Slovak author Emil Svetoň. The board is made up of eight rows numbered 1 to 8 and eight columns, a to h. The notation for describing moves is the same as in chess. There are 36 numbers placed in the middle of the board. The basic principle is that a higher number can jump over a lower number to an empty square (for example, a 7 can jump over a 1, 2, 3, 4, 5 or 6 but not a 7 or an 8). The number which has been jumped over is removed from the board and its value (in points) is written down by the diagram alongside the move itself. The aim of the game is to get as many points as possible in ten moves. Individual jumps (moves) are written down in chess notation. So for the example shown in the diagram, you would write:

1. f6 – h6 (5 points)
2. g4 – g6 (1 point) etc.

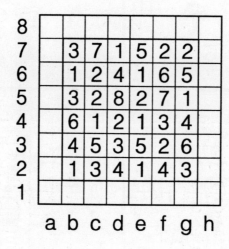

You can use the grids provided to work out your moves. Two have been provided for your convenience. Write your solution in the table:

Move	Points
1.	
2.	
3.	
4.	
5.	
6.	
7.	
8.	
9.	
10.	

Total points:

	a	b	c	d	e	f	g	h
8								
7		4	1	2	6	2	5	
6		2	3	4	1	4	5	
5		1	5	3	8	3	3	
4		7	4	1	2	3	2	
3		6	1	2	4	6	1	
2		7	2	1	1	5		
1								

	a	b	c	d	e	f	g	h
8								
7		4	1	2	6	2	5	
6		2	3	4	1	4	5	
5		1	5	3	8	3	3	
4		7	4	1	2	3	2	
3		6	1	2	4	6	1	
2		7	2	1	1	5		
1								

LIGHTHOUSES

In the sea, represented by a 10 x 10 grid, there are seven lighthouses, each one lighting up a *complete horizontal and a complete vertical strip.* Ten boats, the size of one square, are all lit up by at least one lighthouse. The number on each lighthouse represents the number of boats which the lighthouse has in its beams of light. None of the boats touches a lighthouse or another boat. Find the position of all ten boats. Mark the position of the boats with black circles; water may be marked with crosses.

Example:

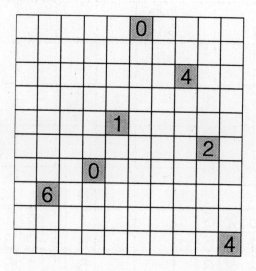

Solution:

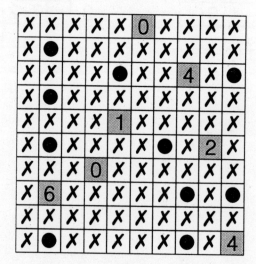

LIGHTHOUSES 1

LIGHTHOUSES 2

Two-Way Anagrams

A make of car is concealed in each row and each column. The letters in the car names do not go one after another in the right order, as this is an anagram. For example, you will find the word FERRARI in the first column. This means that the remaining three letters in the column will be parts of car names in rows A, D, and E. No single letter can be used more than once. For example, the letters from FERRARI are only valid for this vertical word and cannot be used horizontally. As a help in solving, circle all letters from makes of cars concealed horizontally and cross out letters from those concealed vertically. On uncovering the make of a car, write it in the table by the appropriate row or under the appropriate column.

In all, 20 makes of car are concealed in the table. You can find them among the 30 makes below.

Abarth	Mazda	
Alta	Nissan	
Audi	NSU	
Austin	Opel	
Bond	Pontiac	
Dino	Renault	
Ferrari	Rover	
Fiat	Saab	
Ford	Seat	
Holden	Subaru	
Honda	Suzuki	
IFA	Talbot	
Lada	Tatra	
Lancia	Toyota	
Lotus	Volvo	

	1	2	3	4	5	6	7	8	9	10
A	C	O	I	A	L	A	N	D	A	A
B	R	Y	O	T	U	O	B	A	T	V
C	A	U	A	A	A	L	I	D	S	E
D	T	L	Z	U	N	T	N	E	A	R
E	S	F	R	A	B	U	A	A	T	U
F	R	T	I	T	U	T	A	N	S	O
G	R	O	V	T	S	V	O	L	E	R
H	E	H	A	A	O	O	N	L	D	R
I	A	R	M	A	I	B	S	T	A	F
J	R	D	D	R	L	P	A	A	E	O

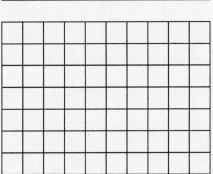

MULTIPLICATION PUZZLE

Fill in the digits 1 to 9 such that the number written above the diagonal of filled-in squares (i.e., the top right-hand corner) is the product of the digits in the empty squares to the right, and such that the number written below the diagonal (i.e., the bottom left-hand corner) is the product of the digits in the empty squares below this number. The digits should be different in each multiplication (none of them should be used twice). As a hint, some of the digits are already filled in.

Example:

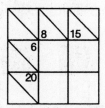 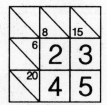

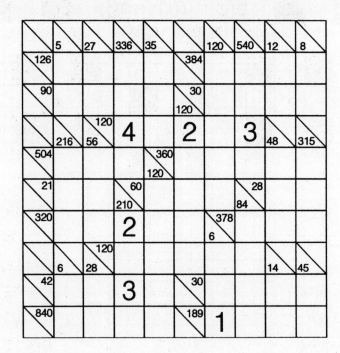

Do You Speak Esperanto?

It doesn't matter at all if you don't. You certainly do know how to solve crisscross. Your task is to fill in this crisscross composed of 36 five-letter words in Esperanto (the letter R is already filled in as a little hint). The six highlighted squares contain the keyword. Even if you are not fluent in Esperanto, you will certainly understand this keyword.

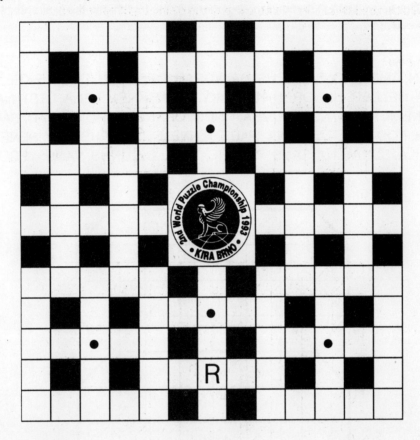

ABELA	KLIFO	OPERO
ABOLI	KRABO	OPONI
ABONO	LARGE	OVALO
ALIAM	LEONA	PARTE
ALIRI	LINCO	PIANO
AROMI	MISIO	PIKOJ
BINDI	MOLEO	PIPRI
BLEKE	NASKA	PRAVA
BOMBO	NEGRO	REVUI
EMIRO	NENIA	SIGMO
JAMBO	OLIVO	STOPI
KABLO	OPALO	TROVI

INTERNATIONAL CROSSWORD PUZZLE

What makes this crossword puzzle interesting is that it is made up of 44 expressions from the 11 languages spoken in the countries whose teams participated in the 2nd WPC. Your task is to put all the expressions into the crossword, going both across and down. Put only one letter into each triangular space. Some of the heavy lines are missing. A four-letter keyword is concealed in the crossword. The heavy lines that you fill in, together with the fact that in the appropriate spots each letter of the keyword appears twice, will help you find the keyword.

AMILYEN, AMIMONO, BACILLUS, BALADRAR, DESEMEN, DEUR, EKEL, ENOM, ESTIMA, HELDER, HUNDRED, KOMICKY, KREM, KREN, LEHA, LEST, NADÁLE, NEIN, NEMI, NEON, NUHA, ODRA, ONDO, ORANGE, ORON, OSAD, PARSEK, PATVAR, PODANIA, RASELINA, RAUB, RINNEN, RUIN, RUSALKY, SENE, SIGN, SILÁ, SUDAMINA, TAUB, TENEKE, TROLLOP, UNUS, VANU, YESO.

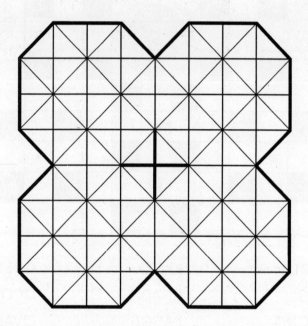

NUMERICAL PENTAMINO

Divide the diagram into nine parts fulfilling the following conditions:

1. Each part must contain five digits;
2. Each part must be a different shape;
3. The sum of the digits in each of the nine parts must equal 17.

7	1	0	5	1	4	7	1	9
3	9	6	1	5	0	6	1	0
4	0	2	2	1	5	4	6	4
0	2	3	6	0	6	8	0	1
3	8	1	5	2	3	5	3	3

EIGHT IS ENOUGH

Insert each of the digits from 0 to 8 into the nine boxes in the given equation, so that the equation holds true. No digit can be used more than once.

55

MONITOR ON THE BLINK

An operation of subtraction is displayed on the computer monitor. The three numbers contain all ten digits from 0 to 9. Each digit is used only once in this subtraction and zero never appears as the first digit in a number. However, the monitor is broken, and so some digits are only partially displayed while some are not displayed at all. Your task is to solve the problem.

The digits:

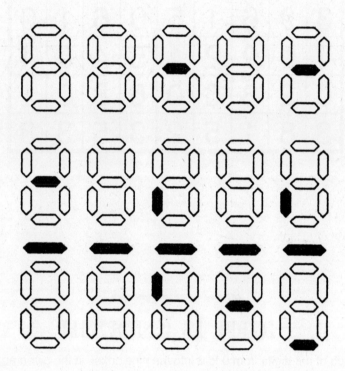

FOUR MOVING POINTS

Each of the eight diagrams is made up of eight circles and is divided into eight sectors. Four points are marked on the diagrams according to a specific system, which is connected to the movement of these points. If you guess the principle behind the movement of the points, you will be able to tell on which circle and in which sector the missing point is located.

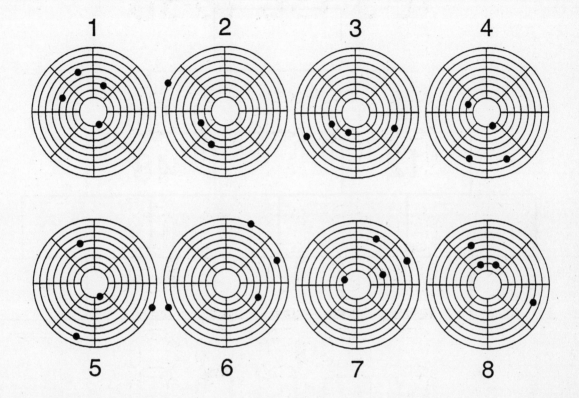

THE MULTIPLICATION PYRAMID

The pyramid is made up of fifteen numbers. Apart from the numbers in the bottom row, each number is the product of the two numbers below it. Fill in the missing numbers.

Example:

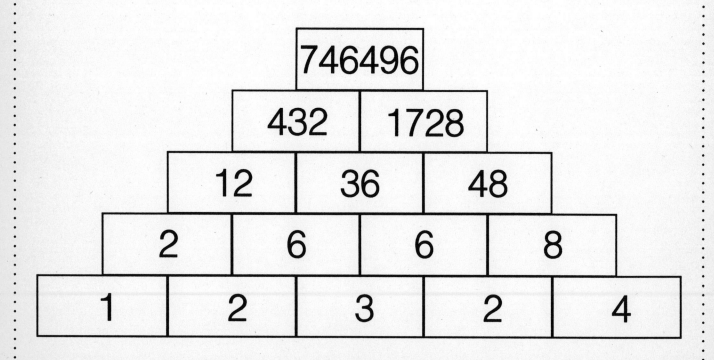

THE MULTIPLICATION PYRAMID

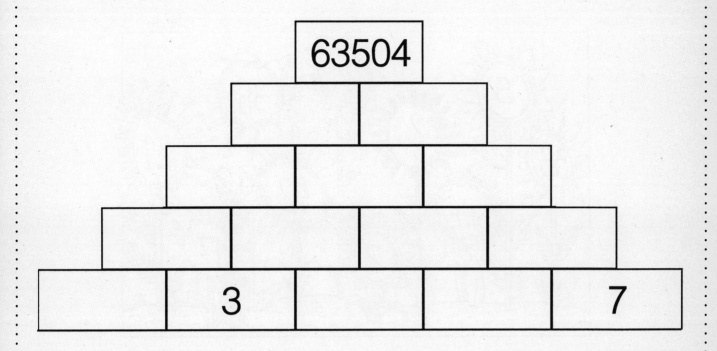

TEN FLOWERS

Twenty different numbers are written on ten flowers, one on each side of each flower. The sum of the two numbers on each flower is always the same and the sum of all ten numbers on the visible side of the flowers equals the sum of the ten numbers on the undersides. What number should replace the question mark?

LADY SINGS THE BLUES

Seven square sections are shown beneath the picture. Mark the positions on the diagram to which these seven sections correspond.

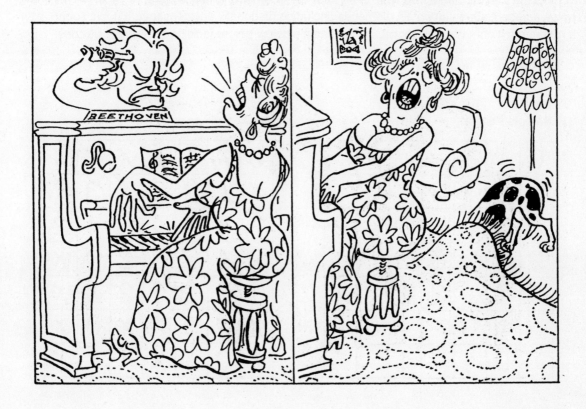

DIAMOND TREASURE

This variation of Minesweeper is played on a 7 x 7 board. There are diamonds hidden in ten of the 49 squares. Your job is to determine their locations. The numbers in the diagram will help you. A number in a square tells you how many diamonds lie next to the square; in other words, how many adjacent squares contain diamonds (including diagonally adjacent squares). No square with a number in it contains a diamond. Try the sample below before tackling the contest puzzles.

Sample Puzzle:

0		1				
		3		3		
	3		4		4	2
2	4		3	2		
1			3	2		
		3			0	
	0			1		

Answers:

0	X	1	X	X	X	X
X	X	◈	3	◈	3	◈
◈	3	X	4	◈	4	2
2	4	◈	3	2	◈	X
1	◈	◈	3	2	X	X
X	X	3	◈	X	0	X
X	0	X	X	1	X	X

DIAMOND TREASURE 1

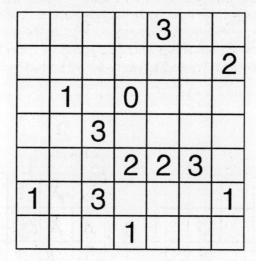

				3		
						2
	1		0			
		3				
			2	2	3	
1		3				1
			1			

DIAMOND TREASURE 2

			2			2
	5					
2		1		0		
			1			
1	2		1			
	1				0	
		1				

		5		4	1	
	2					
				4	2	
	0			3		1
				2	1	
			2			

DIAMOND TREASURE 4

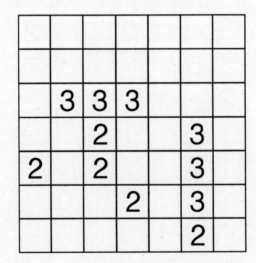

	3	3	3			
		2			3	
2		2			3	
			2		3	
					2	

DIAMOND TREASURE 5

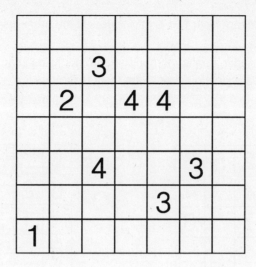

DIAMOND TREASURE 6

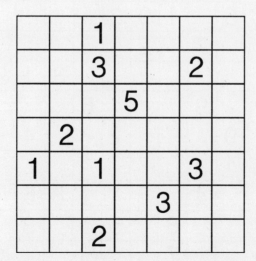

MAGIC SQUARES (CZECH STYLE)

Fill in the squares as follows:

– into square A put the numbers from 1 to 7, into square B the numbers from 1 to 8, and numbers 1 to 9 into square C;

– the numbers should be filled in so that no number appears twice in any one row or column, nor should any number appear twice in either of the main diagonals.

A

1				2	5	3
				4		
		3		7		6
			5			
		4				
6	3	5				7

B

			8		3	2	1
6	8		3			7	
	1	2	6				
8		1			5		
			2	3	7	4	8
3				6			
2							
4				5			

C

5		1	9	3	4			
	7		2					
					3	1	9	
	9			6				
9			2		4			
1		7						
	4		5		1	8	6	
		8		5			3	
		7			5			1

ANAGRAMS 1

Solve these 12 anagrams. Then with the help of the years and
the numbers at the right, solve the "hidden" puzzle.

MAXI COHN	1924	5.
HELMA MILLER	1994	3.
WYLAV SEQUAL	1960	11.
ROB LE MUNE	1956	1.
ROSA POP	1972	3.
EVA L. BILLERT	1992	8.
DICK PAELLA	1932	8.
EGON BREL	1968	1.
JOE VARAS	1984	2.
ED STAMMAR	1928	2.
NEIL KISH	1952	2.
ELLEN SAGOS	1984	3.

ANAGRAMS 2

Solve the 10 anagrams, and find the "hidden" answer.

LOME	+	TARN	=
RENO	+	SAL	=
APO	+	NIL	=
ETNA	+	EHR	=
MONTE	+	DON	=
VINA	+	RIGI	=
BAD	+	AIN	=
MARSALA	+	SADE	=
MAINE	+	ALLE	=
KOLA	+	DAN	=

HOMAGE TO KAFKA

Fill in the three grids using each word below exactly once.

AFRICA	MA
AKUTO	MAINE
ALRAUN	MALAWI
AP	NAMA
APO	NEU
AT	NIAS
EU	NOTA
EWC	OKINAWA
FAKIR	OPALE
FRIA	ORFEO
FRONT	ORIENTE
IMAM	RAIUNO
KAFKA	RHONE
KAFKA	RM
KAFKA	RO
KAREN	RSI
KAU	TP
KAUNA	TRADE
KO	TUTTI
KOM	WORKS

PYRAMID POWER 1

Can you find a continuous path from the top of the pyramid to the bottom,
passing through one block in each level, using each of the 10 digits only once?

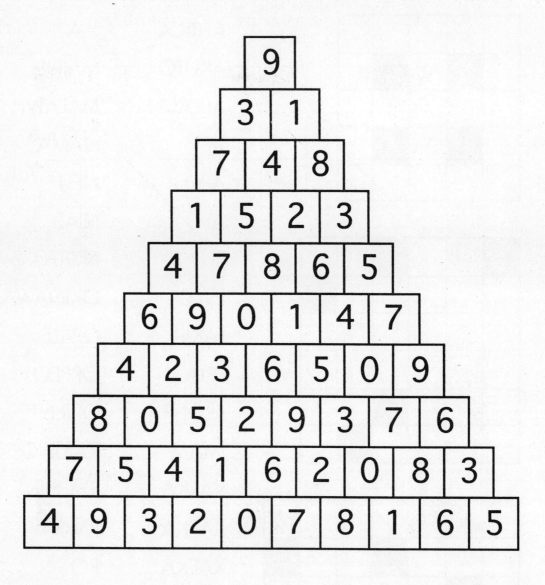

MIRROR, MIRROR

A light bulb has been placed in the corner of this hall of mirrors. If you turned one of the mirrors inside the hall, the beam of light would shine out the exit at the right side. Can you find the mirror to turn?
(The example below shows how the light is reflected within the hall of mirrors;
the mirror you turn should be rotated 90° within its square.)

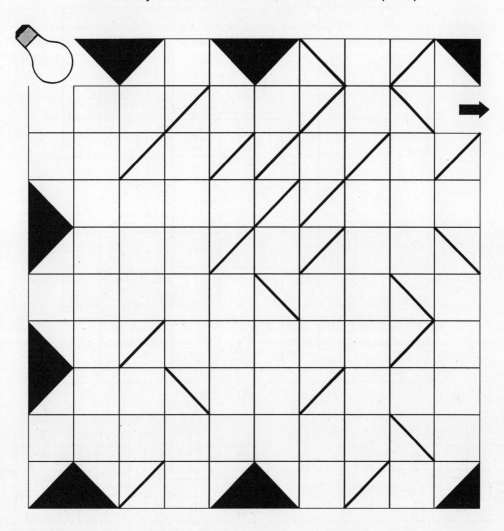

EXAMPLE:

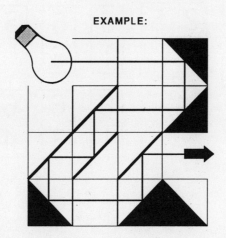

DOMINO THEORY 2

In this puzzle, the dominoes must be placed somewhere in the diagram in the orientations shown below. (They cannot be rotated or reversed.) Each domino will be used once and adjacent dominoes must contain matching numbers.

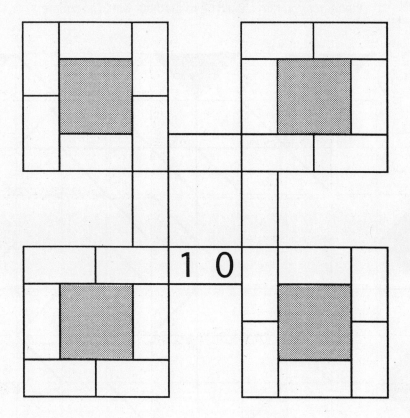

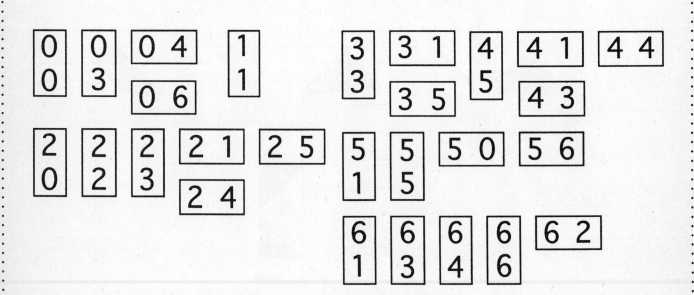

DOWNTOWN THE EASY WAY

Fill in the grid using each city once to find the mystery answer.

ADANA

AVILA

BASEL

BRISTOL

CADIZ

CAPRI

DIJON

KABUL

LHASA

PARMA

PRAHA

SPANDAU

SPLIT

TIRANA

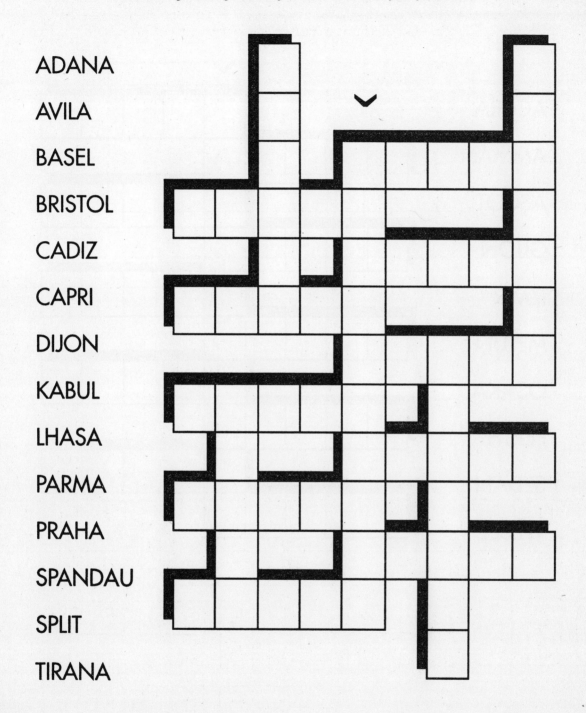

DOWNTOWN THE HARD WAY

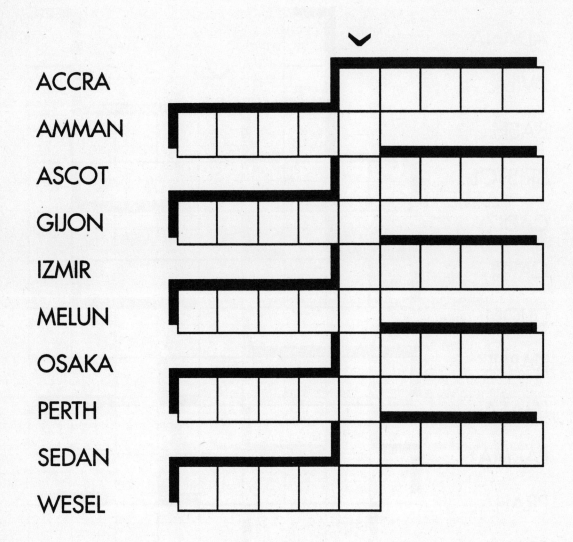

ACCRA

AMMAN

ASCOT

GIJON

IZMIR

MELUN

OSAKA

PERTH

SEDAN

WESEL

Soccer 2

Using the following information, reconstruct the results of the 6 soccer matches below:

The winner of each match gets 2 points.
If there is a tie, each team gets 1 point.
Losers get no points.

STANDINGS

TEAM	GOALS FOR	GOALS AGAINST	POINTS
ATLETICO MANILA	4	0	5
AC MEXICO	2	1	4
FC MOMBASA	1	3	2
DYNAMO MOCKBA	2	5	1

MANILA VS MEXICO   ____ TO ____

MANILA VS MOMBASA   ____ TO ____

MANILA VS MOCKBA   ____ TO ____

MEXICO VS MOMBASA   ____ TO ____

MEXICO VS MOCKBA   ____ TO ____

MOMBASA VS MOCKBA   ____ TO ____

NOT IN MY NEIGHBORHOOD!

Insert the numbers from 1 to 12 into the grid. But be careful! No numbers which are neighbors in the circle are allowed to be neighbors in the grid!

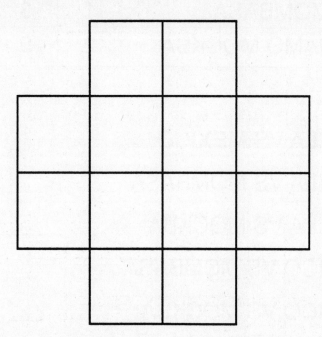

CHAIN GANG

Fill in the grid according to these rules:

Each word entered overlaps 2 letters of an adjacent word (in the same direction).
Intersecting words do not overlap.
One letter to a square regardless.

Example:
ALIBABA
AROMA
LUNA
MANTUA
NATURA
ONTA
OPAL
TATUM

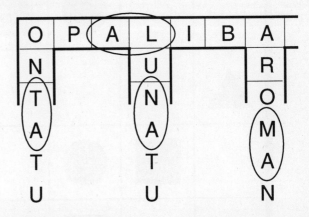

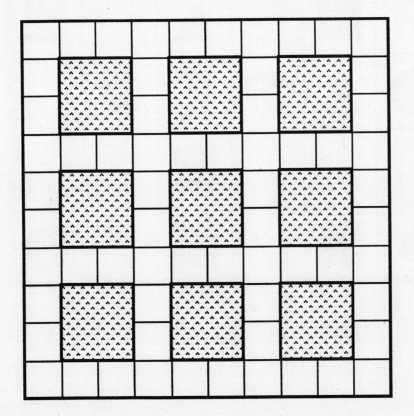

ABERLE
ATOMAR
ARKULES
EMIRAT
ERROL
LESART
MUST
MYOP
OLIM
OPUS
REGA
SPARTE
STOERE
TEPILA
URSOVA
USARMY
VADER
VAMPYR
VIPAR

DIVIDE AND CONQUER

Partition the grid below into four areas, each of the same shape and
each containing two circles, two triangles, and two squares.

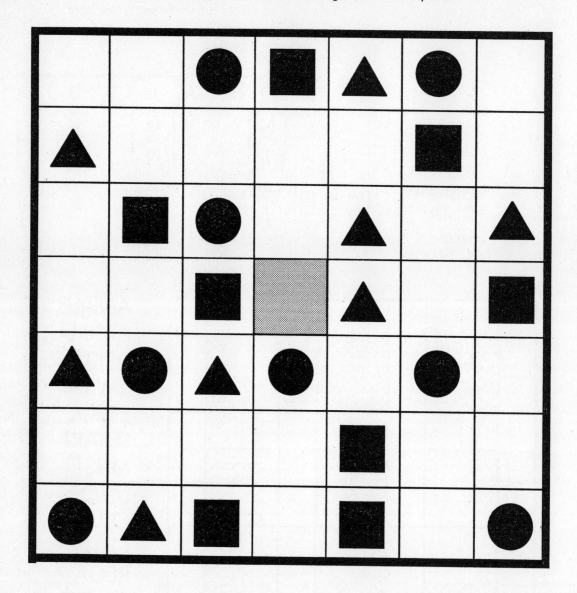

POST OFFICE

Use the numbers in the first grid and a flexible mind in the rest
to help you deduce the missing letters.

Grid 1 (with number labels):

B_1	S_1	R_1	A_4	A_4	N_4
O_1	R_1	B_1	$_4$	E_4	O_4
B_1	K_1	L_1	A_4	V_4	U_4
A_2	I_2	I_2	M_3	E_3	K_3
S_2	$_2$	E_2	R_3	M_3	L_3
O_2	A_2	I_2	G_3	N_3	N_3

Grid 2 (cross shape):

O		A		I
	M	D	M	
O	S	?	K	A
	I	N	H	
M		A		A

Grid 3 (4x4):

?	C	A	L
A	P	M	A
H	G	N	I
K	C	U	B

Grid 4 (5x5):

G	E	N	C	O
O	S	I	N	L
M	I	?	O	R
N	O	O	T	I
R	A	C	N	E

Grid 5 (5x5):

S	H	E	R	L
C	?	N	A	N
?	C	■	K	H
D	?	Y	L	E
?	L	M	E	S

SUMMING UP

Fill in the diagram using each of the numbers 1 to 9
so that adjoining circles sum to the totals shown.

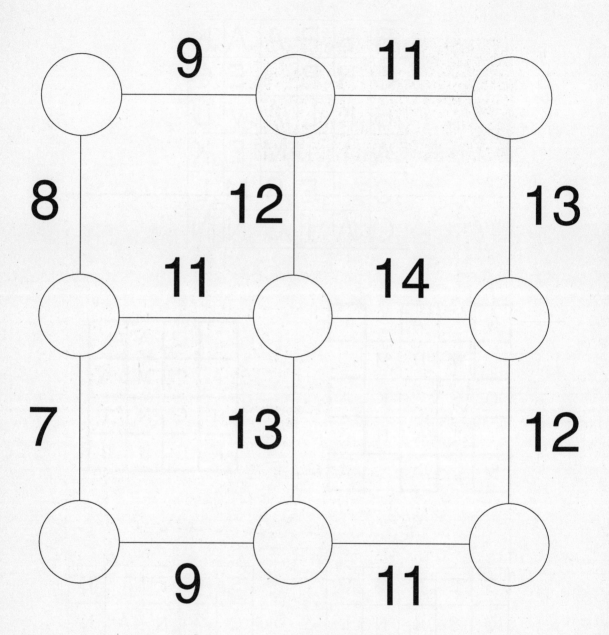

CAR QUEST

Only one of the eight cars in the traffic jam at the bottom of the page matches the white car in every detail. Can you find it?

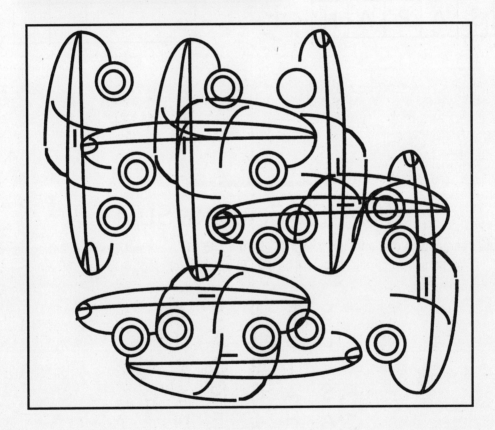

SQUARE SUM

In the word square below, each letter represents a different digit from 0 to 9 in an addition problem. Can you find the unique solution? (None of the five-digit numbers begins with a zero.)

K	A	R	A	S
A	G	O	R	A
R	O	V	E	R
+ A	R	E	N	A
S	A	R	A	H

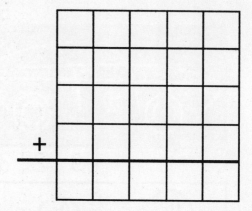

NOT SO SQUARE SUM

Substitute the numbers 0 to 9 for the letters so that the addition is correct. No number begins with 0. When solved correctly you will be able to map the letters to the lines below.

```
  S E P S A
  E S I A H
  P I R O L
+ S A O N E
  A H L E N
```

$$\overline{2\ 6\ 1\ 5\ 0\ 9}$$

$$\overline{7\ 6\ 8\ 3\ 4}$$

PYRAMID POWER 2

Can you find a continuous path from the top of the pyramid to the bottom, passing through one block on each level using each of the 10 digits only once?

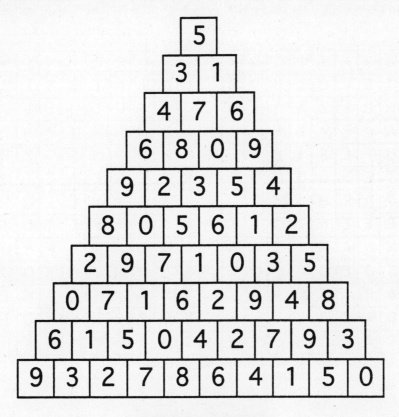

CALLING THE GAME

Five journalists (numbered 1 to 5) predicted the outcome of the placements of five athletes in a competition; the predictions appear in the chart below. No prediction was completely correct, but two journalists correctly predicted the placements of exactly two athletes. The other three journalists were totally wrong. Can you determine the actual outcome of the competition?

	FIRST PLACE	SECOND PLACE	THIRD PLACE	FOURTH PLACE	FIFTH PLACE
1	Ryan	Josemith	Edward	Alonso	Linus
2	Linus	Alonso	Ryan	Josemith	Edward
3	Linus	Josemith	Edward	Alonso	Ryan
4	Edward	Linus	Alonso	Ryan	Josemith
5	Linus	Josemith	Edward	Ryan	Alonso

GIVE 'EM THE WORKS

Reading horizontally and vertically search the grid on the left for major artistic works and the grid on the right for their creators. Match all 28 of them on the chart on the next page. When you are done, the remaining letters will spell out a 29th work of art and its creator.

T	E	B	A	J	A	Z	Z	O	A	Y
N	S	M	O	E	V	D	I	H	D	R
O	A	U	K	L	I	Z	A	A	I	O
N	S	G	A	A	E	M	L	F	A	T
A	I	N	U	F	L	R	I	L	N	S
N	L	O	T	E	I	O	O	N	O	E
T	A	R	T	A	R	H	A	T	R	D
I	N	A	F	E	E	N	T	O	E	I
G	O	Y	N	N	A	N	I	S	B	S
O	M	Z	G	O	E	C	L	C	O	T
N	A	R	A	R	A	A	O	A	A	S
E	I	V	O	M	E	R	L	I	N	E
N	E	M	R	A	C	U	L	U	L	W

L	P	U	C	C	I	N	I	N	I	L	E
V	W	I	N	E	S	B	I	R	E	R	E
O	A	A	C	L	O	E	E	O	A	S	N
K	G	N	H	A	T	P	N	E	E	A	E
O	N	B	B	S	S	C	P	B	Y	N	G
B	E	E	N	E	A	S	I	O	R	O	Z
A	R	R	A	V	E	L	O	I	E	U	O
N	E	G	A	K	E	T	D	T	B	I	L
B	W	L	A	D	E	R	H	O	E	L	A
E	L	H	N	Z	A	E	D	O	W	H	M
O	S	Ä	I	H	I	C	N	I	V	A	D
B	H	B	E	L	L	I	N	I	N	E	B
G	O	L	D	M	A	R	K	N	E	R	N

84

Works of Art	Creators
1.	
2.	
3.	
4.	
5.	
6.	
7.	
8.	
9.	
10.	
11.	
12.	
13.	
14.	
15.	
16.	
17.	
18.	
19.	
20.	
21.	
22.	
23.	
24.	
25.	
26.	
27.	
28.	
29.	

KEEP AWAY

Fill in each sector with the number 1, 2, or 3 so that no like-numbered sectors touch each other.

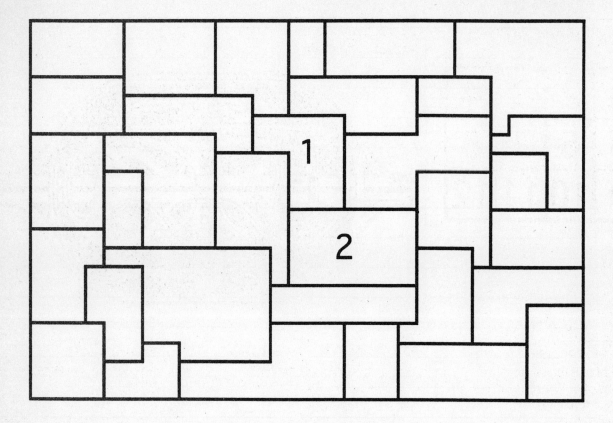

ANSWERS

11 GOING HALFSIES

1	2	3	4
5	6	7	8
9	10	11	12

12 FREEWAY FRENZY

All 6, as shown here

11 TRY-ANGLES

20 (4 of one region, 6 of two regions, 4 of three regions, 4 of four regions, and 2 of six regions.)

12 TIME SHARE

Note: The circled segment remains on for 10 hours without interruption, from 7:00-4:59. The segment below it remains on for only 9 hours without interruption, from 3:00-11:59.

13 COMMON ELEMENTS

1. d (things that have springs)
2. a (things that are red)
3. h (things that drip)
4. f (things that are hollow)
5. g (things that are shaped like letters of the alphabet; note that "c," lying horizontally, does not look like the letter l)
6. e (things that hang)
7. b (things related to night)

14 STEP BY STEP

4-7-2-10-5-8-1-9-6-3

14 DIGITITIS

152,954 (29,826,030 divided by 195)

15 WORD SEARCH

Lima, Peru ("Mali" also accepted in place of "Lima")

15 ROBOT 1

44

15 ROBOT 2

160 (33 units each from the front and back, 21 each from the top and bottom, and 26 from each side)

16 BOXED IN

A, as shown below. (A quick way to solve this without actually making an example is to color each of the pieces like a checkerboard and then note that every piece except "A" has an equal number of dark and light squares; since the 6x6 grid also has an equal number of dark and light squares, "A" can't fit.)

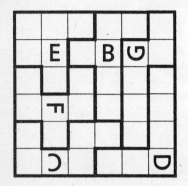

16 TALL TALE

Joyce-Flo-Amy-Kim-Lisa

17 ON OUR HONOR

Top row: A-J-K-Q; second row: J-K-A-Q; third row: K-Q-A-J; bottom row: J-Q-A-K

17 GOING IN CIRCLES

Top row: 1-8-4; middle row: 6-9-3; bottom row: 2-7-5

18 CRISSCROSS

Joan Miro, Paavo Nurmi, Blaise Pascal

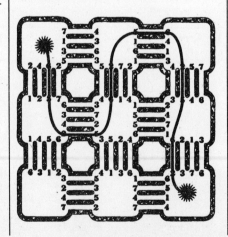

19 A PERFECT MATCH

d-g

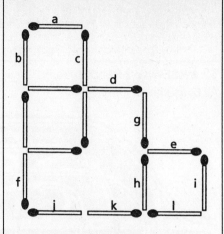

19 SISTER CARRIE

Tom-83; Harry-84; Carrie-85; Dick-86; Brenda-87; Laura-88

20 TRIAL SEPARATION

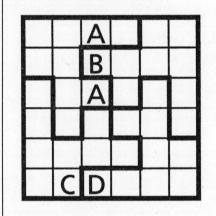

20 KEY DECISION

2-5-6, as shown here

21 SPELLING CHECKER

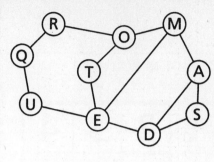

21 TIMES AFTER TIMES

$3 \times 58 = 174 = 6 \times 29$
(or $6 \times 29 = 174 = 3 \times 58$)

22 YEAR'S END

5 (the number of letters that have enclosed parts)

22 CROSS-LINK

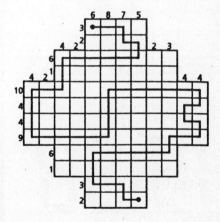

23 PI CHART 1

80, as shown in the upper path shown in first column at the top of the next page.

23 Pi Chart 2

16, as shown in the lower path below

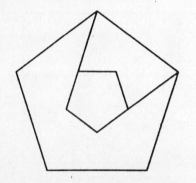

24 Path Marks

4 (A-D-B-E-C-F; A-D-B-F-C-E; A-D-F-C-B-E; and B-F-D-C-A-E)

24 Completely Out Of Shape

8 (one such pattern is shown here)

25 Race For The Gold

The best answer achieved during the competition was 11 words; our best answer (shown below), attained without time constraint, was 12 words. Words used: BIRIR, KRIVELEVA, MARSH, PEREC, PERLOV, ROMANOVA, RUIZ, STUICE, TANUI, TULU, ZELEZNY, and ZMELIK.

RESULTS

The Qualifying Test went to 185 solvers (174 American, 11 Canadian), of whom 171 returned their answers. Contestants ranged in age from 12 to 68, with the average being 29. The highest score on the test was 271 points, the lowest was -85, and the mean was 125. Below are statistics about the number of solvers for each puzzle and whether they solved correctly. Following that is a list of the top 10 American and top 5 Canadian finishers, with their scores. (See page 10 for how to score your test.)

Puzzle	Tried		Right		Wrong	
#	#	%	#	%*	#	%*
1	146	85	137	94	9	9
2	157	92	84	54	73	46
3	151	88	68	45	83	55
4	155	91	97	63	58	37
5	155	91	153	99	2	1
6	166	97	166	100	0	0
7	163	95	163	100	0	0
8	134	78	132	99	2	1
9	145	85	140	97	5	3
10	150	88	146	97	4	3
11	159	93	158	99	1	1
12	138	81	110	80	28	20
13	31	18	25	81	6	18
14	146	85	142	97	4	3
15	160	94	120	75	40	25
16	108	63	36	33	72	67
17	50	29	33	66	17	34
18	138	81	129	93	9	7
19	159	93	136	86	23	14
20	23	13	21	91	2	9
21	61	36	53	87	8	13
22	108	63	105	97	3	3
23	95	56	90	95	5	5
24	53	31	50	94	3	6
25	56	33	46	82	10	18
26	107	63	107	100	0	0
27	18	11	16	89	2	11
28	47	27	34	72	13	28
29	49	29	49	100	0	0
30	111	65	66	59	45	41
31	101	59	62	62	39	39
32	61	36	13	21	48	79
33	69	40	30	43	39	57
34	40		Best: 11 words		Average: 9.05 words	

*Of those contestants who tried the puzzle

Top 10 Americans

	Name	Score	Age	Home/Profession
1	Ron Osher	271	33	Stamford, CT/music executive
2	Dan Johnson	270	28	Terre Haute, IN/software design engineer
3	Wei-Hwa Huang	240	17	North Potomac, MD/high school student
4	Larry Baum	240	41	Bellevue, WA/computer scientist
5	Andrew Brecher	236	19	Lexington, MA/university student
6	Alan Smith	236	36	Hayes, VA/minister
7	Nick Baxter	235	36	Burlingame, CA/director of software development
8	Dave O'Connor	225	23	San Diego, CA/engineer
9	James Wise	213	44	Millwood, WV/electrician
10	Randall Rogers	210	22	Appleton, WI/college student

Top 5 Canadians

	Name	Score	Age	Home/Profession
1	Julian West	236	29	Vancouver, BC/professor of mathematics
2	Ricky Cheung	191	25	Vancouver, BC/computer animator
3	David Samuel	190	31	Montreal, PQ/Ph.D. student
4	Darren Rigby	155	19	Oakville, ON/university student
5	Marie Vasilou	149	23	St. Laurent, PQ/M.Sc. student

The top four solvers in each country won a place on their national teams for the 2nd World Puzzle Championship. The fifth-place solver was the first runner-up.

27 LADYBUGS

27 MINICROSS

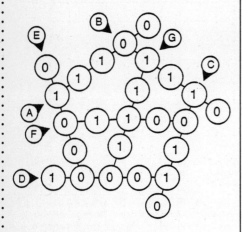

28 PICTURE LOGIC

28 COUNTING SQUARES

92 squares

29 FIND YOUR WAY

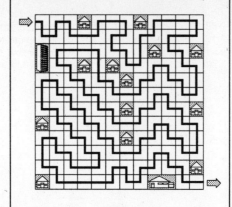

30 SNOWFLAKES

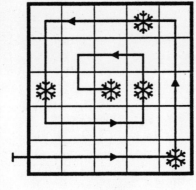

31 DOMINO THEORY I

	6	0		4	1		
3	2	1	1	3	3	1	1
2	4	6	6	5	0	4	1
3	2	1	5	4	5	5	4
0	2	4	6	2	5	6	3
2	0	3	6	0	5	5	3
2	6	0	5	6	0	2	3
	0	4	4	1			

32 FIND THE PAIR

10 and 17

33 TOWN SQUARE

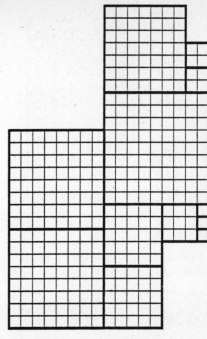

36 BATTLESHIPS 1

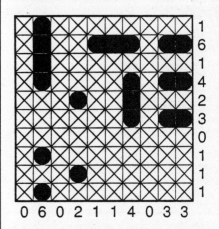

37 BATTLESHIPS 2

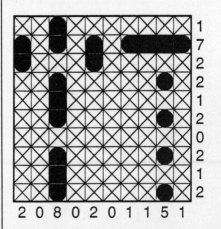

38 BATTLESHIPS 3

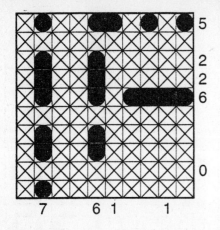

7 6 1 1

5
2
2
6
0

39 BATTLESHIPS 4

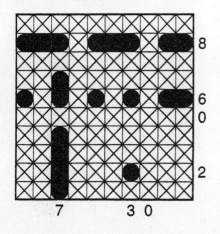

7 3 0

8
6
0
2

40 LOGICAL LABYRINTH

1	2	7	16	5	19	7	8
10	17	23	9	21	13	6	23
15	4	22	17	20	4	18	22
19	17	11	24	3	17	8	19
12	9	7	14	23	18	12	6
6	5	23	14	10	5	2	23
8	20	10	11	19	18	1	17
2	24	15	22	13	4	4	25

41 SWIMMERS

2, 7, 5, 8, 6, 4, 1, 3

42 LEAVES

43 READER

D, I, F, A, C, H, E, G, B

44 SOCCER 1

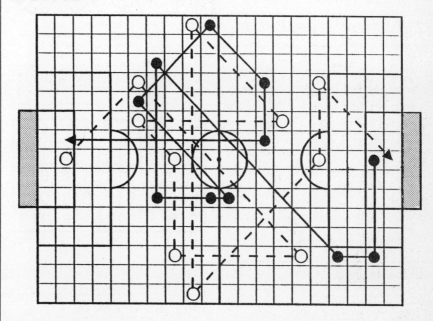

45 HOW MANY?

2 objects (telephone and banana)

47 JUMPING

Our best:

1.	d6-d8	2 points
2.	b4-d6	5 points
3.	d6-f8	6 points
4.	f8-h6	5 points
5.	e5-g7	4 points
6.	h6-f6	5 points
7.	g7-e5	7 points
8.	e5-c5	3 points
9.	b2-b4	6 points
10.	c5-c3	7 points
	Total	50 points

49 LIGHTHOUSES 1

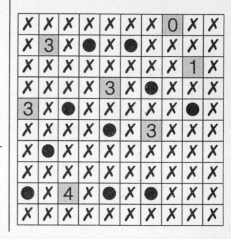

50 LIGHTHOUSES 2

91

51 TWO-WAY ANAGRAMS

	1	2	3	4	5	6	7	8	9	10
A	C	O	I	A	L	A	N	D	A	A
B	R	Y	O	T	U	O	B	A	T	V
C	I	U	A	A	A	L	I	D	S	E
D	T	L	Z	U	N	T	N	E	A	R
E	S	F	R	A	B	U	A	A	T	U
F	R	T	I	T	U	T	A	N	S	O
G	R	O	V	T	S	V	O	L	E	R
H	E	H	A	A	O	O	N	L	D	R
I	A	R	M	A	I	B	S	T	A	F
J	F	D	D	R	L	P	A	A	E	O

LANCIA
TOYOTA
AUDI
RENAULT
SUBARU
AUSTIN
VOLVO
HONDA
FIAT
OPEL

F	F	M	T	N	T	S	L	S	R
E	O	A	A	S	A	A	A	E	O
R	R	Z	T	U	L	A	D	A	V
R	D	D	R		B	B	A	T	E
A		A	A		O				R
R						T			
I									

52 MULTIPLICATION PUZZLE

5	27	336	35		120	540	12	8
126 1	9	2	7	**384**	2	4	6	8
90 5	3	6	1	**30** / **120**	3	5	2	1
216 / **56**	4	5	2	1	3		**48**	**315**
504 9	8	7	**360** / **120**	1	4	9	2	5
21 3	7	**60** / **210**	3	4	5	**28** / **84**	4	7
320 8	1	2	4	5	**378** / **6**	7	6	9
6 / **28**	5	1	3	2	4		**14**	**45**
42 1	7	3	2	**30**	3	1	2	5
840 6	4	7	5	**189**	1	3	7	9

53 DO YOU SPEAK ESPERANTO?

The keyword is **ENIGMO**.

```
K A B L O ▪ O ▪ P R A V A
R ▪ L ▪ P I P R I ▪ L ▪ B
A B E L A ▪ O ▪ K L I F O
B ▪ K ▪ L I N C O ▪ A ▪ N
O P E R O ▪ I ▪ J A M B O
▪ A ▪ E ▪   ▪   ▪ L ▪ I ▪
T R O V I ▪   ▪ P I A N O
▪ T ▪ U ▪   ▪   ▪ R ▪ D ▪
N E N I A ▪ E ▪ M I S I O
A ▪ E ▪ B O M B O ▪ T ▪ V
S I G M O ▪ I ▪ L E O N A
K ▪ R ▪ L A R G E ▪ P ▪ L
A R O M I ▪ O ▪ O L I V O
```

54 INTERNATIONAL CROSSWORD PUZZLE

The keyword is **BRNO**.

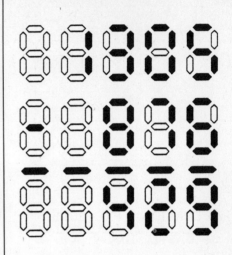

56 MONITOR ON THE BLINK

1305 − 876 = 429

55 NUMERICAL PENTAMINO

7	1	0	5	1	4	7	1	9
3	9	6	1	5	0	6	1	0
4	0	2	2	1	5	4	6	4
0	2	3	6	0	6	8	0	1
3	8	1	5	2	3	5	3	3

59 THE MULTIPLICATION PYRAMID

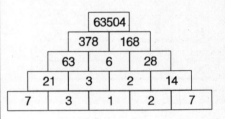

```
        63504
      378   168
    63    6    28
  21    3    2    14
 7    3    1    2    7
```

55 EIGHT IS ENOUGH

3 2⁴ = 1 0 4 8 5 7 6

$$32^4 = 1048576$$

57 FOUR MOVING POINTS

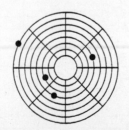

60 TEN FLOWERS

37

The sum of the 2 numbers on each flower is 50, the sum of all 10 numbers on each side is 250.

61 Lady Sings The Blues

66 Magic Squares (Czech Style)

A

1	4	7	6	2	5	3
7	2	6	3	4	1	5
4	1	3	5	7	2	6
5	7	1	4	6	3	2
3	6	2	1	5	7	4
2	5	4	7	3	6	1
6	3	5	2	1	4	7

B

5	6	7	8	4	3	2	1
6	8	4	3	2	1	7	5
7	1	2	6	5	8	3	4
8	7	1	4	6	2	5	3
1	5	6	2	3	7	4	8
3	4	5	7	1	6	8	2
2	3	8	5	7	4	1	6
4	2	3	1	8	5	6	7

C

5	2	1	9	3	4	6	7	8
6	7	4	2	9	8	1	5	3
7	5	6	8	4	2	3	1	9
8	9	3	4	1	6	5	2	7
9	8	5	1	2	3	7	4	6
1	3	2	7	6	9	4	8	5
3	4	9	5	7	1	8	6	2
2	1	8	6	5	7	9	3	4
4	6	7	3	8	5	2	9	1

63 Diamond Treasure 1

63 Diamond Treasure 2

64 Diamond Treasure 3

64 Diamond Treasure 4

65 Diamond Treasure 5

65 Diamond Treasure 6

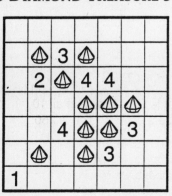

67 ANAGRAMS 1

CHAMONIX	=	O
LILLEHAMMER	=	L
SQUAW VALLEY	=	Y
MELBOURNE	=	M
SAPPORO	=	P
ALBERTVILLE	=	I
LAKE PLACID	=	C
GRENOBLE	=	G
SARAJEVO	=	A
AMSTERDAM	=	M
HELSINKI	=	E
LOS ANGELES	=	S

68 ANAGRAMS II

MONTREAL	=	M
ORLEANS	=	O
NAPOLI	=	N
TEHERAN	=	T
EDMONTON	=	E
VIRGINIA	=	V
IBADAN	=	I
DAR ES SALAAM	=	D
EL ALAMEIN	=	E
OAKLAND	=	O

69 HOMAGE TO KAFKA

70 PYRAMID POWER 1

9, 1, 4, 5, 8, 0, 3, 2, 6, 7

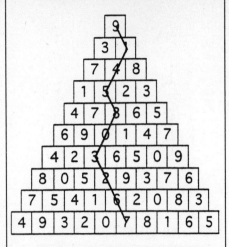

71 MIRROR, MIRROR

The mirror that must be turned is circled below.

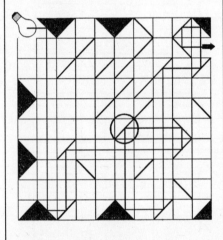

72 DOMINO THEORY 2

73 DOWNTOWN THE EASY WAY

74 DOWNTOWN THE HARD WAY

75 SOCCER 2

Manila vs. Mexico	0 to 0
Manila vs. Mombasa	2 to 0
Manila vs. Mockba	2 to 0
Mexico vs. Mombasa	0 to 0
Mexico vs. Mockba	2 to 1
Mombasa vs. Mockba	1 to 1

76 NOT IN MY NEIGHBORHOOD!
Here is one possible solution:

	1	10	
11	6	3	8
2	9	12	5
	4	7	

77 CHAIN GANG

V	A	D	E	R	R	O	L	I	M
I		M		I		P		U	S
P	A	B	E	R	L	E	S	A	R	T
A		R		A		A		R	O
R		K		A		R		R	E
U	R	S	O	V	A	M	P	Y	R	E
L		E		M		A		Y	O
E		O		A		Y		O	G
S	P	A	R	T	E	P	I	L	A

78 DIVIDE AND CONQUER

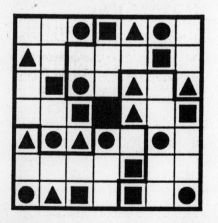

79 POST OFFICE
Missing letters are
2. O
4. N
A, E, L and four O's

80 SUMMING UP

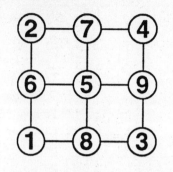

81 CAR QUEST
The matching car is shown in black below.

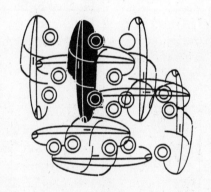

82 SQUARE SUM

```
    2 1 3 1 9
    1 7 8 3 1
    3 8 5 6 3
 +  1 3 6 0 1
  ─────────────
    9 1 3 1 4
```

82 NOT SO SQUARE SUM

```
    2 3 1 2 9
    3 2 0 9 5
    1 0 8 6 7
 +  2 9 6 4 3
  ─────────────
    9 5 7 3 4
```

S	O	P	H	I	A		L	O	R	E	N
2	6	1	5	0	9		7	6	8	3	4

83 CALLING THE GAME
First place-Edward; second-Alonso; third-Ryan; fourth-Linus; fifth-Josemith

83 PYRAMID POWER 2
5, 1, 7, 8, 3, 6, 0, 9, 2, 4

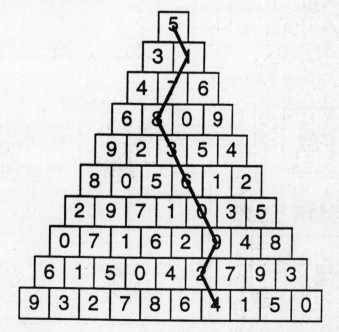

84 GIVE 'EM THE WORKS

Aida – Verdi, Giuseppe
Antigone – Anouilh, Jean
Bajazzo – Leoncavallo, Ruggiero
Bolero – Ravel, Maurice
Carmen – Bizet, Georges
Dafne – Peri, Jacopo
Eroica – van Beethoven, Ludwig
Eva – Lehár, Franz
Ezio – Händel, Georg Friedrich
Faust – Goethe, Johann Wolfgang von
Fiorenza – Mann, Thomas
Guernica – Picasso, Pablo
Hamlet – Shakespeare, William
Lakme – Delibes, Leo
Lohengrin – Wagner, Richard
Lolita – Nabokov, Vladimir
Lulu – Berg, Alban
Merlin – Goldmark, Karl
Mona Lisa – da Vinci, Leonardo
My Fair Lady – Shaw, G. Bernard
Nana – Zola, Émile
Nanon – Genee, Franz Friedrich R.
Nero – Boito, Arrigo
Nora – Ibsen, Henrik
Norma – Bellini, Vincenzo
Oberon – Weber, Carl Maria von
Tosca – Puccini, Giacomo
West Side Story – Bernstein, Leonard
= Evita – Lloyd Webber, Sir Andrew

86 KEEP AWAY

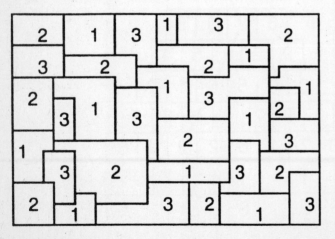

CREDITS

U.S./CANADA QUALIFYING TEST

Page/Puzzle	Author
11. Going Halfsies	Nob Yoshigahara
11. Try-Angles	Mary Gabriels
12. Time Share	John Chenesky
12. Freeway Frenzy	Steve Ryan
13. Common Elements	
Set 1	Will Shortz
Set 2	Will Shortz
Set 3	Robert Leighton
Set 4	Will Shortz
Set 5	Will Shortz
Set 6	Will Shortz
Set 7	Will Shortz
14. Step By Step	Peter Gordon
14. Digititis	Peter Gordon
15. Word Search	Will Shortz
15. Robot 1	Peter Gordon
15. Robot 2	Peter Gordon
16. Boxed In	Mike Shenk
16. Tall Tale	Bob Stanton
17. On Our Honor	Mary Gabriels
17. Going In Circles	Ogden Porter
18. Crisscross	Peter Gordon
19. A Perfect Match	Will Shortz
19. Sister Carrie	Bob Stanton
20. Trial Separation	Rodolfo Jurchan
20. Key Decision	Steve Ryan
21. Spelling Checker	Will Shortz
21. Times After Times	Nob Yoshigahara
22. Year's End	Ogden Porter
22. Cross-Link	Guney Mentes
23. Pi Chart 1	Will Shortz
23. Pi Chart 2	Will Shortz
24. Path Marks	Steve Ryan
24. Completely Out Of Shape	Will Shortz
25. Race For The Gold	Will Shortz

SECOND WORLD PUZZLE CHAMPIONSHIP

The puzzles on pages 27 through 66 are courtesy of Vitezslav Koudelka, editor-in-chief of Kira Publishing Co., Brno, Czech Republic.

THIRD WORLD PUZZLE CHAMPIONSHIP

The puzzles on pages 67 through 86 are courtesy of Andreas Franz, chief puzzle editor of Bastei-Verlag, Bergisch Gladbach, Germany.

If You Like This Book, You'll Love The Magazine!

Subscribe to **GAMES** magazine. Get six issues a year for just $19.97. Satisfaction guaranteed or 100% of your money back.

☐ **Bill me later**   ☐ **Payment enclosed**

Name
_____
Please Print
Address
_____
                                    Apt. No.
City/State/Zip

Please allow 4-6 weeks for delivery. Canadian orders: $24.97 for 6 issues.
All other foreign orders: $29.97 for 6 issues pre-paid in U.S. currency.

G6RHC

Subscribe to **GAMES** magazine. Get six issues a year for just $19.97. Satisfaction guaranteed or 100% of your money back.

☐ **Bill me later**   ☐ **Payment enclosed**

Name
_____
Please Print
Address
_____
                                    Apt. No.
City/State/Zip

Please allow 4-6 weeks for delivery. Canadian orders: $24.97 for 6 issues.
All other foreign orders: $29.97 for 6 issues pre-paid in U.S. currency.

G6RHC

Subscribe to **GAMES** magazine. Get six issues a year for just $19.97. Satisfaction guaranteed or 100% of your money back.

☐ **Bill me later**   ☐ **Payment enclosed**

Name
_____
Please Print
Address
_____
                                    Apt. No.
City/State/Zip

Please allow 4-6 weeks for delivery. Canadian orders: $24.97 for 6 issues.
All other foreign orders: $29.97 for 6 issues pre-paid in U.S. currency.

G6RHC

If You Like This Book, You'll Love The Magazine!

GAMES